T0316670

Cambridge Elements ☰

Elements in Shakespeare Performance
edited by
W. B. Worthen
Barnard College

PERFORMING EARLY MODERN DRAMA BEYOND SHAKESPEARE

Edward's Boys

Harry R. McCarthy
Jesus College, University of Cambridge

CAMBRIDGE
UNIVERSITY PRESS

CAMBRIDGE
UNIVERSITY PRESS

University Printing House, Cambridge CB2 8BS, United Kingdom

One Liberty Plaza, 20th Floor, New York, NY 10006, USA

477 Williamstown Road, Port Melbourne, VIC 3207, Australia

314–321, 3rd Floor, Plot 3, Splendor Forum, Jasola District Centre, New Delhi – 110025, India

79 Anson Road, #06–04/06, Singapore 079906

Cambridge University Press is part of the University of Cambridge.

It furthers the University's mission by disseminating knowledge in the pursuit of education, learning, and research at the highest international levels of excellence.

www.cambridge.org
Information on this title: www.cambridge.org/9781108810234
DOI: 10.1017/9781108893848

© Harry R. McCarthy 2020

First published 2020

A catalogue record for this publication is available from the British Library.

ISBN 978-1-108-81023-4 Paperback
ISSN 2516-0117 (online)
ISSN 2516-0109 (print)

Performing Early Modern Drama Beyond Shakespeare

Edward's Boys

Elements in Shakespeare Performance

DOI: 10.1017/9781108893848

First published online: October 2020

Harry R. McCarthy

Jesus College, University of Cambridge

Author for correspondence: Harry R. McCarthy, hrm65@cam.ac.uk

ABSTRACT: This Element provides the first in-depth study of the present-day all-boy company, Edward's Boys, who are based at King Edward VI School ('Shakespeare's School') in Stratford-upon-Avon. Since 2005, the company has produced a wide array of early modern plays, providing the most substantial repertory of early modern drama available for examination by scholars. The Element provides a comprehensive account of the company's practices, drawing on extensive rehearsal and performance observation, evidence from the company's archive, and interviews with actors and key company personnel. The Element takes account of the company's particular educational and strongly interpersonal environment, suggesting that these factors have a distinctive shaping force on their performance practice. In the hands of Edward's Boys, the Element argues, early modern drama becomes the source of company creation, ensemble practice, and virtuosic physical play, inviting us to reimagine what it means – and takes – to perform these plays today.

KEYWORDS: boy actors, early modern drama, theatre company, Shakespeare, Edward's Boys

ISBNs: 9781108810234 (PB), 9781108893848 (OC)

ISSNs: 2516-0117 (online), 2516-0109 (print)

Contents

Introduction

A performance of *Henry V* at the Royal Shakespeare Company's Swan Theatre (Stratford-upon-Avon) in 2013. The lights came up on the academic--gowned Chorus (Tim Pigott-Smith) marking exercise books at an Elizabethan-style desk. Two schoolboys, in regulation navy-and-gold blazers and ties, thundered onto the stage, stopping in their tracks as they met 'Sir's' gaze. The Bishops of Canterbury and Ely – played, again, by two teenage boys – began their opening exchange. Two boys of more diminutive stature (dressed in the army fatigues of the Combined Cadet Force and waving cricket bats aloft) gave chase through the audience; and on the performance went, with more and more schoolboys filling the stage: a roguish, rugby-thug of a Bardolph with long socks trailing around his ankles; an adolescent Henry (complete with prefect badge) delivering his Harfleur speech from the top of a rugby line-out (see Figure 1). The elderly Pigott-Smith aside, the 'happy few' of this production were schoolboys through and through.

On the surface, this production of *Henry V* by the boys of King Edward VI Grammar School (KES) seems the most conventional of places to begin an Element in the Shakespeare Performance series. KES, after all, is the school Shakespeare himself is thought to have attended; and, in many ways, the production's impetus was conventional indeed, serving to mark the centenary of a performance of the same play by boys from the same school.[1] An all-boy production of Shakespeare's great paean to English military prowess certainly made sense in 1913. The 2013 production was, however, a rather different story. The company who took to the stage in this centenary production was, after all, not just any group of boys, but Edward's Boys, an amateur troupe composed entirely of pupils (aged 11–18) from the school which has been in continuous operation since 2008. Born initially out of a series of short scenes from early modern school plays filmed for Michael Wood's *In Search of Shakespeare* series (BBC2, 2003) and followed a year later by a sequence of workshops on early modern cross-dressing led by Carol Chillington Rutter, this company does not, as a rule, *do* Shakespeare. Instead, as their website states, they 'strive to explore the repertoire of the boys' companies' under the direction of the school's deputy headmaster, Perry Mills (*Edward's Boys*).

---

[1] Piggott-Smith was himself an 'Old Boy' of KES.

Figure 1 Jeremy Franklin as Henry V and the Edward's Boys ensemble in the 2013 production of Shakespeare's *Henry V*, directed by Perry Mills. Photo by Gavin Birkett, courtesy of Edward's Boys.

Though a relatively new company, Edward's Boys has a densely layered history. Over a twelve-year period, the troupe has mounted full-scale productions of plays by Francis Beaumont, Thomas Dekker and John Webster, John Ford, Ben Jonson, John Lyly, Christopher Marlowe, John Marston, Thomas Middleton, and Thomas Nashe, in addition to shorter entertainments by the Tudor schoolmaster John Redford and the Caroline university playwright Charles May.[2] These productions constitute the largest corpus of early modern boy theatre in performance available for examination by twenty-first-century scholars, having been performed at the grammar school as well as on tour in venues as varied as Oxford college dining halls, the Sam Wanamaker Playhouse, St Paul's Cathedral, a chapel in Montpellier, and a ducal palace in Genoa.[3] So extensive and varied is their

---

[2] See the Appendix for a full timeline of productions.

[3] A full archive of performances, recorded on DVD, is available for purchase from the company's website.

repertory, in fact, that Andy Kesson is surely right to suggest, in a review of the company's 2018 production of John Lyly's *The Woman in the Moon*, that the boys have worked with plays by 'a more impressive range of early modern dramatists than any other theatre company has managed . . . including early modern theatre companies themselves' ('Women in the Moons').

By the time the company came to stage *Henry V*, then, their track record was not one of Shakespeare performance but of performing Marston's *The Dutch Courtesan* and *Antonio's Revenge*, extracts from Lyly's *Endymion* and *Mother Bombie*, Middleton's *A Mad World, My Masters* and *A Chaste Maid in Cheapside*, and, most recently, Dekker and Webster's *Westward Ho!*. As I discuss in this Element, these unique productions had been distinctly shaped by the company's institutional context and their development of a vigorous, contemporary performance style. I argue throughout that, in the hands of Edward's Boys, early modern drama becomes a site of sport and play, of physical experimentation, and of exploring contemporary boyhood. As my brief description at the outset of this Introduction suggests, the performance of *Henry V* was no different. Regular followers of Edward's Boys may, for instance, have recognised some of the overtly boyish set pieces from previous productions: the schoolboy choristers returning from the opening of *A Chaste Maid in Cheapside* (2010), the reckless throwing of props and furniture from the punk-infused *A Mad World, My Masters* (2009), the virtuosic sword fights and the tiny body of the Boy held cradled in Henry's arms repeating similar sequences in *Antonio's Revenge* (2011). Then there were the actors themselves: I would venture that there is no other actor than Edward's Boys' Jeremy Franklin to have played Henry V off the back of performing as Mistress Birdlime in *Westward Ho!*, Duke Piero in *Antonio's Revenge*, and Lady Kix in *A Chaste Maid in Cheapside*. In recycling similar motifs, costumes, and acting personnel, this production was, in Marvin Carlson's term, significantly 'haunted' (Carlson 8). The ghosts evoked here were not, however, recent stagings of Shakespeare's other plays but of works which had been virtually unstaged in the professional or amateur repertory for four centuries.[4]

---

[4] In the Appendix, I provide brief performance histories, including details of recent revivals, for each Edward's Boys play.

Embedding *Henry V* within a wide-ranging non-canonical repertory was certainly the approach taken by company director Perry Mills:

> I wanted to say, 'we don't do Shakespeare – what is the point when he didn't write for boys?' But I didn't say that because it would have been ungracious ... So it just stayed there for about a year – probably getting on for two years, where I was thinking, how the hell am I going to do *Henry V* with a bunch of schoolboys *in the Swan*? ... And then I realised the obvious thing. They're just boys ... Almost every production we've ever done in some way relates to education ... The whole thing about education and school uniform and learning about history and lessons and on and on and on just fed through the whole thing. So actually the answer to that is that eventually we worked on it in exactly the same way as we do another one ... the things that we had by that stage learned about early modern drama we just applied to that play, without thinking 'oh my God, it's Shakespeare'. There was no fear of that at all ... Was I conscious of adopting a different approach? I really wasn't. I was worried about that, and then I realised that that was silly. I shouldn't be worried about it – just do it as a play. (personal interview, 2020)

For Mills and the company, the anxieties concomitant with performing *Shakespeare* were eventually allayed by the decision instead to perform *company*: 'It was sort of like "let's pretend nobody's ever done *Henry V*, and we'll do our take on it"' (personal interview, 2020). As Peter Kirwan put it in his review of the production, audience members were consistently invited 'to see the school performing itself haphazardly and playfully', a playfulness which 'kept in mind the youth of the participants, the war always to some extent a sport' ('Review: *Henry V*'). Subjecting the Shakespearean text to the shaping force of the company's 'usual' way of working enabled Edward's Boys to perform the play 'in exactly the same way as we do another one'.

In this Element, I explore the rehearsal and performance practices, born out of the company's important institutional contexts, that have given rise to a mode of production that makes it possible to 'just do' anything from *Mother Bombie* to *Henry V* 'as a play'. I argue that, for Edward's Boys, the guiding principle for the exploration of early modern drama through performance is one dominated by a mode of production which is infiltrated by the rhythms of school life and a collective, ensemble-based approach to practical experimentation. Even in the case of a play as canonical as *Henry V*, Edward's Boys provide a model of early modern performance in which the authorial text is vigorously reshaped by the company's distinctive identity: a wide-ranging, multi-authored repertory; an intensely collaborative approach to rehearsing and performing; and shared understandings and systems of behaviour. This identity, I suggest, can help us embark on Kirwan's project of developing 'a vocabulary of performance for early modern drama that shifts away from the all-pervasive Shakespeare filter' ('Not-Shakespeare' 100). Part of the value of Edward's Boys lies in their work's potential to help us tell an alternative story of early modern drama in contemporary performance to one dominated by Shakespeare-centrism and the primacy of the authorial text.

Though the company has amassed a significant following illustrious enough to include Royal Shakespeare Company (RSC) directors,[5] this Element constitutes the first detailed study of Edward's Boys. I provide a comprehensive account of the company's origins, their rehearsal process, and their performances in order to think more carefully than has been typical about how the company's working practices help to shape a distinctive anti-canon of early modern dramatic performance. Given the Boys' ever-increasing popularity in UK academic and theatrical circles,[6] it is

---

[5] Gregory Doran, for instance, is enough of a fan to be able to recall roles that certain actors played years ago. Among the many documents held in the company's archive at KES – of which more in this section – is an undated letter sent to Mills after the production of *A Trick*, in which Doran recounts, 'I think the Courtesan was your Galatea, and I am certain I have seen Lucre before' ('Comments'). Doran was right on both counts – Charlie Waters played Galatea in 2014, and, by the time he played Lucre in *A Trick*, Joe Pocknell had performed in six Edward's Boys productions.

[6] The company's website provides enthusiastic testimonials by the likes of theatre historians Laurie Maguire and Tiffany Stern and Shakespearean actors such as

surprising that to date the work of Edward's Boys has received relatively little scholarly attention aside from reviews of individual productions.[7] Scholars have occasionally engaged with Edward's Boys productions in their readings or performance histories of specific plays, in preparing new editions of writers such as Webster, or in wider discussions of the performance and transmission of early modern drama.[8] However, a deeper exploration of the company's work and what it tells us – or prompts us to ask – about early modern plays in performance by boy actors has yet to be written.

To this end, between 2018 and 2020 I undertook a detailed study of the company's operations from its origins to the present day, comprising extended visits to the company's archive, based in KES's Memorial Library, which contains uncatalogued holdings, including private correspondence, production sketches, scripts, and rehearsal schedules (as well as the odd bloody handkerchief or false cigarette). Surveyed in full, the archive provides ample scope to reconstruct a narrative of mounting Edward's Boys productions from casting to initial rehearsal to final performance. I have supplemented this narrative with analysis of numerous Edward's Boys productions, viewed live or on DVD. These performances show these archival traces in action and, most importantly, allow us better to understand how the company's performances of these historically under-performed plays distinctly reshape the texts for today's audiences. The ensemble nature of Edward's Boys' operations which is so demonstrably central to their performances is arguably best understood by speaking to the actors themselves: I therefore draw on the testimonies of a dozen actors who have performed in multiple company productions between 2010 and 2020, as

Anton Lesser, and the Boys are regularly invited to contribute to large-scale academic projects such as the Thomas Nashe Project and the forthcoming Oxford Marston. For more information on these projects, see *The Thomas Nashe Project* and *The Complete Works of John Marston*, respectively.

[7] A notable exception is the work Carol Chillington Rutter carried out with the company in the early years of its formation – see Section 1.

[8] See Aebischer, *Screening* 172–3, 228–9, 232, 238–42, 248, 250; Britland 75; Gunby, Carnegie, and Jackson 163–4; Maguire and Smith 184–6.

well as Mills himself.[9] Throughout the study that follows, I am interested in how the company values and institutional dynamics that so demonstrably run through their practice intertwine productively with the early modern playtexts on which they base their performances. As the brief sketch of the company's *Henry V* has shown, this intertwining of practice and text is possible and productive even when it comes to the most canonical of plays, and it is my contention that we have much to gain from attending to such a dynamic in our study of early modern drama, Shakespearean and non-Shakespearean, in performance.[10]

Taking my cue from recent studies of how the work of individual companies and theatre practitioners contributes to the landscape of contemporary Shakespeare performance emblematised by Bloomsbury's Shakespeare in the Theatre series (see 'Shakespeare in the Theatre'), I suggest that the work of Edward's Boys allows us to take a large corpus of neglected early modern drama on Shakespearean terms, to consider it with the same level of seriousness, the same level of contemporaneity. Given their considerable experience of performing early modern drama as a cohesive company with an established set of working practices, Edward's Boys provide an important counterpoint to the Shakespeare-dominated companies on which the Bloomsbury series largely focuses (the non-Shakespearean productions by Cheek by Jowl and the American Shakespeare Center explored by Peter Kirwan and Paul Menzer

---

[9] To provide a sense of the actors' longevity and varied experience with the company, when introducing each of them I give details of all of the roles they have played in an accompanying footnote.

[10] It is worth stating at this point that my extensive work on this company has of necessity meant I have developed a close working relationship with the actors and particularly their director. In addition to multiple archival visits, rehearsal observations, and joining the company on tour around the UK, I have frequently socialised with Mills and have provided additional (though not financial) support to the company through assistance with advertising, providing costumes, producing a podcast about the cancelled 2020 production of *The Silent Woman* (see Appendix), and, in one happy turn of events, teaching an Edward's Boys alumnus who embarked on a degree at my university. It is my hope in the discussion that follows that my obvious enthusiasm for the company's work, and my close proximity to their operations, does not compromise the critical insights I offer.

notwithstanding). Taken as a collective output, the company's work occupies a significant place on the map of non-Shakespearean early modern performance charted in Pascale Aebischer and Kathryn Prince's excellent *Performing Early Modern Drama Today* – a book whose 2012 publication came rather too early to discuss the work of Edward's Boys in more than a single footnote.[11] Given the company's longevity and consistency in personnel – many company members appear in multiple productions throughout their time at school – the wide-ranging repertory of Edward's Boys offers greater scope for detailed exploration than the standalone productions, script-in-hand readings, or research-based exercises discussed by Aebischer and Prince's contributors.

In what follows, then, I am above all concerned with what Edward's Boys has to tell us about what it means (and takes) to perform non-Shakespearean early modern drama today, as well as what such practices might mean for performing Shakespeare. I begin by situating the company within a recent performance tradition interested in early modern drama's 'historical recovery'. Here, I chart the company's gradual progression from its initial interest in the 'authentic' performance of gender to the development of a cohesive ensemble. Retaining the company's all-male ensemble even as KES has begun to accept girls into the school's Sixth Form has made it necessary for boys to continue playing women;[12] nevertheless, in recent years the company has moved further and further away from prosthetic gender performance. I suggest, however, that their rejection of 'authentic' performance practices does not lessen the value of their exercises in historical (re)performance: paradoxically, their contemporary approach to early modern drama strengthens their connections to the performances of the past.

Having critically defined the nature of the Edward's Boys project, I move more specifically to consider a central feature of their work on early modern plays – engaging closely with the authorial text. Though beginning with the text is obviously not unique to Edward's Boys, I demonstrate how from their earliest rehearsals the boys are trained to engage not only with the author's

---

[11] See Heron, Monk, and Prescott 162.

[12] In the British school system, pupils in the Lower Sixth Form (or Year 12) are typically aged between sixteen and seventeen; those in the Upper Sixth Form (Year 13) between seventeen and eighteen.

language but with the text's implicit prompts for movement. In their text work, I argue, Edward's Boys reshape the words of the author through the body. The benefits of this approach become all the more clear when the actors begin to 'put the text on its feet' in the studio rehearsals later in the production process. In my discussion of these rehearsals, I centralise the boys' acts of taking 'ownership' of the play and its performance through physical experimentation. Here, I draw on my own observations of the company working through dense and knotty moments in rarely staged plays and particularly on their collaborative work with freelance movement director Struan Leslie to suggest that watching the company in the rehearsal room can alert us to the shaping effect collaborative, moving bodies can have on our sense of early modern drama's physical potential. The Edward's Boys rehearsal room, I suggest here, is a space in which the past and its performances can be re-encountered through the body.

In the final section, I consider how the Edward's Boys repertory is shaped not only by close attention to text and movement but also – and perhaps especially – by the company's distinctive institutional contexts. The company has fostered an intensely collaborative and self-iterating way of working since its formation through a continual emphasis on approaching performance as sport. I argue that the company's stage work is indelibly shaped by its basis in an elite grammar school which provides ample opportunity for sports practice and, concomitantly, by the ethos of healthy competition, teamwork, and camaraderie such an environment fosters in its pupils. Through these contexts, Edward's Boys have developed a distinctive repertoire of non-textual and non-theatrical practices which directly contribute to the company's performances of early modern drama, and I conclude by suggesting that increasing our awareness of such contexts can greatly enhance our appreciation of the productions to which they give rise.

1 From Prosthetics to Practice: Forming a Company

It is worth beginning by acknowledging the distinctly Shakespearean impetus for the company's founding. In the early 2000s, the historian and broadcaster Michael Wood was preparing a four-part BBC2 series centred on Shakespeare's life and work, titled *In Search of Shakespeare*. Wood's examination of Shakespeare's early life, in the second episode titled 'A Time of Revolution', naturally brought him to King Edward VI School, Stratford-upon-Avon's (then all-boy) grammar school which Shakespeare most likely attended. Wood's interest in the school was piqued when he came into contact with Perry Mills, an English teacher and the school's deputy headmaster, who had long been involved with the production of KES's theatricals. At Wood's request, Mills agreed to contribute to the section of the programme which dealt with Shakespeare's education in the classics by rallying some of his pupils to produce a series of short scenes from Elizabethan schoolroom interludes, as well as some of the Latin orations by the wronged women of classical literature that he almost certainly would have studied. The brief scenes featuring the present-day schoolboys repeatedly emphasised their historicity in their attempt to gain access to the educational environment which, according to the series' tidy sweeping narrative, ignited Shakespeare's passion for the theatre. One sequence depicts a boy in a flowing red wig being daubed with red lipstick by one of his peers, while another shows one of the actors being unlaced from an 'authentic' women's gown on loan from the RSC. Despite the ostensible focus on Shakespeare at school, the documentary's use of Shakespeare's young successors gave equal weight to that most tantalising of 'Shakespearean' practices: boys playing women.

It is clear that, for Mills, the success of the enterprise was hampered by the application of period dress and make-up as a means to access the theatrical practice of the past. So much so, in fact, that when *In Search of Shakespeare* aired, entire sequences in which some of the boys dragged up to perform women's laments from Ovid's *Heroides* were cut entirely. In a filmed interview with the theatre historian Carol Chillington Rutter produced several years later, he comments,

> It kind of worked, but it wasn't good enough. There was a boy who was fourteen, who I'd chosen deliberately because he had a bit of acting talent, and I knew he wouldn't be fazed by playing female roles. But in the end the challenge proved too much for him, and it probably proved too much for me as well. It was the first time I'd ever tried to

direct a boy playing a woman's part, and it was *very*
theatrical . . . Up the other end [of the schoolroom] we set
up a little make-up table, and the costume he wore was
gorgeous, and the make-up and wigs all came from the RSC,
and although it was set up as though a boy was making his
schoolmate up, it wasn't the case at all: it was an RSC make-
up person . . . It was all artificial, and everything was very
elaborate: 'look, he's playing a woman, so we'll put lots and
lots of eyeliner, and lipstick' . . . That may or may not
approximate what happened in the Elizabethan theatre, but
what it did for that boy was it just overwhelmed him with
make-up and costume, and he never really found what he
was supposed to be doing. ('The Boy Players – Extended')

Mills's comments are revealing in that they speak back to a considerable
body of work, already well developed by 2003, which engages with
historical performance practices as a means to gain access to what
W. B. Worthen terms the 'original theatrical force' of Shakespeare's plays
(*Force* 29). This work has often incorporated boy actors and the all-male
stage into its purview, particularly within what has come to be known as
'Original Practices' (OP), a term that was coined in the first decade of the
twenty-first century by Mark Rylance during his tenure as the first artistic
director of Shakespeare's Globe in London. Though interpreted in various
ways by scholars, in the main, 'OP' describes attempts to reconstruct, to the
best of practitioner knowledge and ability, the original performance conditions of the early modern theatre. In this, OP performances often seek to
create a shared understanding among actors and audiences that '"this is how
and where it was done"' (Conkie, *The Globe Theatre Project* 290). Despite
the popularity of the fifteen OP productions staged at Shakespeare's Globe
up to 2005, OP's ability to shed critical light on early modern performance
practice has rightly met with scepticism. Don Weingust, for instance,
argues that in their highly selective nature – the use of immediately obvious
historical elements such as costume and music – OP productions frequently
reveal themselves to be more 'performances of authenticity' than 'authentic
performances' (405). In its fetishisation of the material past, the use of the

grammar school boys in *In Search of Shakespeare* became one such 'performance of authenticity', falling prey to what Alan C. Dessen has termed 'theatrical essentialism' and suggesting an unbroken continuity between past practice and present meaning (46).

Mills's comments suggest that the use of authentic materials ultimately had a constricting effect on the performances of these twenty-first-century actors rather than allowing participants and viewers to gain a greater level of access to the performances of Shakespeare's schoolfellows. Instead of releasing the 'original theatrical force' of the early modern stage, they arguably barred access to it altogether, stopping the performance in its tracks and suffocating it under lace and taffeta. For Rutter, the use of KES boys in the BBC2 series endorsed a 'theatrical fallacy', co-opting easily recognisable historical materials as a means of 'seeing into' early modern practice ('Learning Thisby's Part' 11–12). Rightly dissatisfied with the documentary's limiting focus on 'Shakespearean' cross-dressing, Rutter approached Mills shortly after it had aired to invite him to develop a new project on early modern boy performance. This project, though still focused on the prominent cross-dressing question, would be unencumbered by the pursuit of authenticity. Titled 'The Thisby Project', Rutter's work with Mills and the boys of KES turned away from the restaging of 'a mass cultural impression of the Shakespearienced present in "fancy dress" borrowed from the past' ('Learning Thisby's Part' 11). Instead, the focus of the project was on the concept of transvestism as 'textual affect', culminating in a filmed performance of extracts from Shakespeare's plays and their source texts (Ovid's *Heroides* and *Metamorphoses*). This feature of Shakespeare's work, which Rutter and the boys sought to explore, lay not in the clothes that animate the performances but 'in the rhetoric' ('Learning Thisby's Part' 11, 9).

Over the course of 'The Thisby Project', a handful of boys at various stages in their school careers worked with Mills and Rutter on a number of Shakespearean scenes. What united the extracts was their explicit focus on gender impersonation and, in particular, the performance of women's suffering: Julia/Sebastian describing her/his experience of acting the woman's part in *The Two Gentlemen of Verona*, Viola/Cesario's unwitting wooing of Olivia in *Twelfth Night*, Cleopatra's histrionics at Antony's departure and her abuse of the messenger who brings her news that he is married. The performance concluded, 'just for fun', with two extracts from the boy company's investigation of gender construction par excellence, Jonson's *Epicene*.

The project was an intentional departure from much academic theorisation about the erotic nature of gender impersonation in the early modern period. Rutter defines the aim of the project as an interrogation of

> what academic writing had been telling us for the past dozen or
> so years about 'erotic politics' on the early modern stage –
> 'erotics' most provocatively signalled, perhaps, in the mischie-
> vous title to Stephen Orgel's 'Nobody's Perfect – or – Why
> did the English stage take boys for women?' Specifically, we
> wanted to investigate how actors in Shakespeare's (and
> Jonson's and Middleton's) all-male theatre played the woman's
> part by simulating their experience, conducting experiments in
> cross-dressing. ('Playing with Boys' 101)

Throughout the 2005 DVD film of the final performance (titled *Elizabethan Boy Players*), what is emphasised is not the artificial construction of femininity but the rhetorical nature of gender impersonation and women's experiences. This focus is signalled from the very start of the performance. The DVD recording opens with a boy in his mid-teens (Oliver Hayes) standing in the centre of the performance space – the school's preserved Tudor classroom in a nod to the project's Shakespearean impetus – dressed in 'stage blacks' over which is laid a long rehearsal skirt. His face free from the framing of a wig, his hair worn conventionally short, he slowly delivers Arthur Golding's translation of Ovid's letter from Ariadne to Theseus, reading the speech from a leather-bound volume but nevertheless holding the audience's attention with a steely, rueful gaze. His broken voice is unaltered, and he takes his time as he reads from the page, following the punctuation's rhetorical assistance and taking mid-line breaths, stressing the iambs, forcing the dentals and plosives, and pointing up the line endings and routine rhyming couplets. As Ariadne's lament becomes more desperate, so too does Hayes's delivery: he quickens the pace, allowing lines to run on from one another and moving higher up his vocal register. As his voice becomes more urgent, so too does Ariadne: the text becomes overlaid with emotion, particularly its vocatives – 'Why?' – which he shouts out front. His voice begins to crack and soften, and tears spring to his eyes as he wends his way towards the speech's conclusion.

What is brought to the forefront in this performance's rejection of external gendered accoutrements is the textual affect of femininity: his stirring speech is inflected by powerful rhetorical delivery which is nevertheless the product of the body and voice of a schoolboy. Throughout her introductions of scenes from Shakespeare's plays, included on the DVD recording, Rutter routinely draws attention to the verbal dynamics of the scenes in question which animate the character's experience: the 'mobility of thought process' that animates Olivia's back-and-forth pursuit of Cesario/Viola, the excessive rhetorical forms that allow Cleopatra to mount such a terrifying attack on her messenger. While this focus may seem textually dominated to the point of effacing the boys' performances, the absence of excessive 'staginess' in the form of cosmetic overlay paradoxically serves to deepen their physical engagement with the scenes. Rutter endorses this reading in her reflections on the project several years later, by which point the company proper was beginning to form and had staged full-length plays by Marston and Middleton, as well as extracts by Lyly, with some participants on 'The Thisby Project' featured in the cast.[13] As she puts it, divesting the boys (quite literally) of expectations of visual authenticity left them 'able to concentrate on the hard business of making the script work' ('Playing with Boys' 103).

Rutter's observations of the project are somewhat romantically framed: she describes 'The Thisby Project' as 'a total immersion course in emotional literacy' which 'licensed lubberly lads to explore, to own "girly feeling"', for instance ('Playing with Boys' 102). Her insistence on the need to depart from the 'theatrical fallacy' of cosmetic authenticity nevertheless marks an important stage in the development of Edward's Boys. Mills has since recounted to me

[13] Tom Adams, Jack Fielding, and Oliver Hayes, all of whom took both male and female roles in the 2005 workshops, appeared in *The Dutch Courtesan* (Fielding and Hayes), *A Mad World, My Masters* (Adams, Fielding, and Hayes), and *A Chaste Maid in Cheapside* (Fielding and Hayes). Hayes made an unusual return to the company for Charles May's *Grobiana's Nuptials* in 2016, six years after he had left school.

that during the 2005 workshops he had little sense that the boys' exploration of early modern drama would go any further (personal interview, 2018). However, from 2008, a series of opportunities to perform non-Shakespearean plays in collaboration with the University of Warwick (where Rutter is Professor of Shakespeare and Performance Studies) and the Education Department at Shakespeare's Globe quickly began to present themselves. By the 2009 performances of *A Mad World, My Masters*, Edward's Boys was formed.[14] While every play the company has performed since then has featured prominent women's roles, however,[15] the implications of boys playing women have consistently taken a back seat. For one thing, no extant play from the early modern period requires every actor in the cast to take on the role of a woman: indeed, of the 159 boys who have appeared in one or more Edward's Boys productions, only 58 – or 36 per cent – have played a woman. Of those 58, 27 – or 47 per cent – have played women on multiple occasions, with some degree of specialisation. A recent cast member, Ritvick Nagar,[16] has noted that in casting productions 'there's normally a go-to prostitute' (personal interview), and some actors, such as Charlie Waters (see Note 19), are known among the company for their particular 'line' in cross-gender performance.

It is clear from the actors' testimonials that, for them, playing a woman is simply one task among many in the staging of an early modern play. At a 2011 talk given by prominent cast members at a school in Oxford, George Matts drew

---

[14] Mills recalls coming up with the name on the bus ride to Warwick's CAPITAL centre where the boys were performing that evening (personal interview, 2018).

[15] The only exception is Thomas Nashe's *Summer's Last Will and Testament* (2017).

[16] Nagar has appeared in twelve Edward's Boys productions: as a mute in Ford's *The Lady's Trial* (2015); Lazarillo's boy in Beaumont's *The Woman Hater* (2016); Thomas More in the 2016 showcase *Unperfect Actors*; Pamphagus in *Grobiana's Nuptials* (2016); a creditor and Lady Foxtone in Middleton's *A Trick to Catch the Old One* (2017); Ver in *Summer's Last Will and Testament* (2017); Feliche from *Antonio and Mellida* and Pandulpho from *Antonio's Revenge* in a Research in Action event on the works of Marston at Shakespeare's Globe in 2017; Stesias in Lyly's *The Woman in the Moon* (2018); Ver from *Summer's Last Will* in the 2018 showcase *When Paul's Boys Met Edward's Boys*; Mendoza in Marston's *The Malcontent* (2019); Confidence and Honest Recreation in Redford's *Wit and Science* (2019); and Truewit in *The Silent Woman* (2020).

on his experiences of performing as Moll in *A Chaste Maid in Cheapside* a year earlier to describe the company's approach in refreshingly pragmatic terms:

> How does a boy play a female role? What he doesn't do is don false breasts and adopt a high voice. Indeed, we have found the unnerving effect of a deeper-voiced 'woman' only serves to empower the role, as well as heightening the levels of self-consciousness in its playing. We feel the answer is: play the character as one would any other. ('Script for Talk' n.p.)

For Mills, too, the notion of boys playing women is 'really not a problem. Edward's Boys don't attempt to impersonate women. They're not illusionists. They're actors playing parts. It's simply a question of ACTING – or perhaps I should say PLAYING. They aren't kings or generals or murderers either yet they play these roles' ('In the Company' 279). This rationale, which stridently steers clear of the vexed question of 'passing' as a woman on the twenty-first-, or indeed seventeenth-, century stage, has consistently had a notable effect on the design of the company's productions. This is not to say that certain actors have entirely rejected parodied gestures of grotesque or matronly femininity when it suited the tone of the piece. The older women who feature in several of the plays the company has performed have routinely received such treatment, particularly when played by older and larger members of the company: Barnaby Bos's twinsetted, handbag-clutching Alice in the 2013 *Henry V*, James Wilkinson's nasal-voiced lascivious Nurse in Marlowe and Nashe's *Dido, Queen of Carthage* (2013), and James Williams's burly Deaf Gentlewoman in Beaumont's *The Woman Hater* (2016) all deliberately and parodically pointed to the young man beneath the costume. Meanwhile, certain casting choices have given way to remarkably convincing impersonations: George Hodson, who played Princess Katharine in *Henry V*, was apparently taken for a 'real' girl by a number of audience members.[17] As a rule, however, stock gestures and coded performance conventions rarely feature on the company's stages and in their rehearsal rooms (see Figures 2 and 3). This is

---

[17] Actor Dan Wilkinson recalls this audience response in a documentary film made about the company's production of *Dido, Queen of Carthage* and posted to *Vimeo* (see *Performing Dido*).

so much the case, in fact, that, when the RSC's movement director, Struan Leslie,[18] was brought in with the specific aim of teaching the boys to move 'as' women, he quickly found the task to be redundant. 'It is profoundly interesting to me', he writes in a programme note for the company's 2014 production of Lyly's *Galatea*,

> that the work which I thought would take up most of my time – that of helping the boys play girls – is usually a minor

Figure 2 David Fairbairn as Venus, in conversation with production designer David Troughton backstage at Christ Church College, Oxford, during the 2013 production of Christopher Marlowe and Thomas Nashe's *Dido, Queen of Carthage*, directed by Perry Mills. Photo by Richard Pearson, courtesy of Edward's Boys.

[18] At the time of writing, Leslie has worked on eleven of the company's productions (see Section 3).

Figure 3 Charlie Waters as Julia in the 2016 production of Francis Beaumont's *The Woman Hater*, directed by Perry Mills. Photo by Mark Ellis, courtesy of Edward's Boys.

part of my remit. I help and support, but unlike cross-gender work with adult actors there needs to be little exploration. Boys bring to these plays an openness that is more fluid and unfettered than an adult company when men are portraying women. Sometimes this may have an air of pantomime about it; and sometimes it stills an audience like nothing else. You never know where you are with boys. ('Moving Lyly')

The company is under no illusion that these choices and their effects can tell us anything 'concrete' about the practices and dynamics of historical performances: more important to them is the successful navigation of the playtext's demands and opportunities. As in the 2005 cross-dressing workshops, it is therefore far more common to find the boys making little attempt to conceal their biological sex beneath excessive costume. In *Antonio's Revenge*, for instance, every member of the cast wore a school uniform beneath a standard-issue boiler suit, adding token elements such as wigs and long skirts to indicate the femininity of Mellida (Harry Bowen), Maria (Alex Lucas), and Nutriche (Henry Edwards). As Peter Kirwan comments in his review of the production, 'rather than draw attention to the young bodies of the actors, or the cross-gender casting, the actors simply played the characters straight', meaning that '[t]he cross-dressing was an unremarkable aspect of the production, rather than pointed up as unusual or transgressive' ('Review: *Antonio's Revenge*'). Some pragmatic habituation to particular costumes is, of course, occasionally required. For Charlie Waters, who has performed multiple women's roles for the company,[19] an ease in heels is of

---

[19] Waters performed in twelve company productions between 2013 and 2018: as the Boy in *Henry V*; Ascanius in *Dido, Queen of Carthage*; Galatea in *Galatea*; Castanna in *The Lady's Trial*; Julia in *The Woman Hater*; a singer in the one-off 2016 performance of scenes from *Richard II* titled *Will at Westminster*; Grobiana in *Grobiana's Nuptials*; the Courtesan in *A Trick to Catch the Old One*; Orion in *Summer's Last Will and Testament*; Alberto from *Antonio and Mellida* and Andrugio from *Antonio's Revenge* in the Marston Research in Action event; Learchus in *The Woman in the Moon*; and Pandora (from *The Woman in the Moon*) and Dido (from *Dido*) in *When Paul's Boys Met Edward's Boys*.

great benefit – and, having been decked out in a Marilyn Monroe wig and patent leather stilettos as Julia in *The Woman Hater*, he should know. While he 'couldn't actually tell people how to be a woman', 'the only thing I could say . . . is just to practise in heels – so, a week before the performance, in every rehearsal, you just walk around in heels' (personal interview).

Practice clearly pays off: one of the congratulatory emails collated by Mills after the 2019 *Malcontent* describes being 'struck by the fact that the actors who wore high heels automatically took on what code to us as feminine gestures and motion, and that the way their shoulders, hips, and legs became repositioned to suggest female form even without false breasts' ('Emails'). For this viewer, the actors seem to have been little more than a way to 'road test' contemporary preconceptions of gender performance. It is important to stress, however, that the company's approach to women's roles does not attempt to engage questions of verisimilitude *or* parody. Walking adeptly in high heels or finding the right wig to frame one's face certainly can produce a remarkably convincing woman; but the performance of femininity does not constitute a separate strand, or even a particularly central aspect, of the company's practice. Instead, it is inextricably intertwined with what Rutter calls 'the hard business of making the script work' ('Playing with Boys' 103).

Despite the company's pragmatic approach, it is worth stressing that audiences are continually fascinated by the question of 'how' the boys 'play women' (as though there can ever be one fixed answer). This is presumably one of the reasons why the company continues to operate as an all-boy outfit, despite the reduced focus on gender impersonation and regardless of the fact that KES has not been an all-boy school since 2013.[20] For the past seven years, girls aged sixteen to eighteen have been admitted to the school's Sixth Form, and some of these girls have occasionally taken part in Edward's Boys productions as stagehands or, in the case of John Ford's *The Lady's Trial* (2015), as silent members of the onstage audience. Though set up at a time when the school was not co-educational, Edward's Boys is now a single-sex operation within a mixed-sex environment. In this light, it is perhaps difficult to square their rejection of 'authentic' performance practices with their obvious – and deliberately engineered – commercial

---

[20] See 'Admissions Policy'.

appeal as an all-boy company. This all-male dynamic is also maintained at the level of the repertory: without exception, all of the plays the company has performed have been male-authored. There are obvious reasons for this: a writer like Aphra Behn is too late, and no other early modern woman wrote a boy company play. Nevertheless, it is worth bearing in mind that the company's homosociality and reification of an all-male ideal extend beyond its cast. I mention this not to criticise Edward's Boys, their repertory, or their recruitment processes but simply to demonstrate to the reader that the company's structure is now a matter of choice rather than necessity – a point I will return to in Section 4.

It would no doubt be of great interest to consider the effects a mixed cast would have on any production of an Edward's Boys play: indeed, the inclusion of girls in the cast might help to extend further academic engagement with the gender politics of these plays beyond questions of 'believability' or parody. My wish in this Element to move beyond questions of gender (here, cross-dressed performance) is not to suggest that I believe that all has been said on the matter in terms of the company's composition or its productions. As Emma Smith cautions, simply suggesting that biologically male actors acting women's roles in the present is uniformly accepted or unremarkable is hardly a satisfactory 'clarification through the empirics of performance' (qtd. in Carroll, Smith, and White 56). I agree with Smith that such a critical move more likely constitutes 'a loss, a retreat from interesting, politically engaged criticism about gender and sexuality and topics which matter now, and which we can get at and have a forum for via these plays' (qtd. in Carroll, Smith, and White 57). Nevertheless, I suggest that an excessive focus on the implications of Edward's Boys playing women provides a limiting filter through which we can access their approach to early modern drama and the ways in which their productions make meaning in the present. In any case, given the age of the company's actors, and the fact that all of them are very much still alive, to dwell at length on this interpretive lens poses a not inconsiderable ethical dilemma.

Questions of recruitment aside, I have found it necessary to dwell on this feature of the company's practices at such length in order to reiterate the extent to which the company's focus has continually shifted away from gendered material prompts and, thus, from the taint of 'authentic' or 'original' practice that has haunted performance-based exploration of early modern drama both inside and outside of the academy. As Mills himself describes,

> The original focus of the project – boys as girls – has shifted. Subsequently, we explored the repertoire of the boys' companies, but now the interest primarily rests in the educational power of this model. An extraordinary, self-regulated process of apprenticeship, whereby the younger members of the company learn as much from the older performers as they do from me, is now the primary focal point. ('In the Company' 283)

If gendered performance is no longer the vehicle for the company's exploration of early modern drama, a study of Edward's Boys needs to look considerably further than cosmetic attempts to force present-day practice to 'tell' us something about the past and, particularly, beyond gender impersonation. After all, even ridding the boys of the kinds of costumes which overwhelmed the young actors preparing for Wood's documentary in 2003 was clearly not enough to initiate a sustained engagement with the demands and opportunities presented by performing early modern drama today. Indeed, anyone familiar with the productions that the company have mounted since 2009 could be forgiven for failing to recognise *Elizabethan Boy Players* as forming part of the Edward's Boys project (indeed, four of the actors involved in the workshops did not go on to appear in any subsequent productions). The piecemeal performances of Shakespearean and Jonsonian scenes are decidedly different from the physically dynamic stagings such as that of *Henry V* discussed in the Introduction to this Element. Erotically charged scenes such as Antony and Cleopatra's parting in act one, scene three, for instance, are remarkably, unhelpfully, chaste, impeded by awkward gapping between performers and a bashful lack of physical contact. Recalling those early workshops, Mills, too, sets them apart from the company as it is now:

> even then I didn't feel it was going to lead anywhere, and it was very much pulling in people that I had worked with, in

> some cases quite a lot, on various other kinds of plays …
> I don't think I came up with, 'right, this is Edward's Boys, so
> we've got to work a different way'. But we hadn't cohered as
> a company. (personal interview, 2018)

Today, the coherence of the company, and the emphasis it places on mutual knowledge exchange and shared learning opportunities, constitutes the central tenet of its operations. As the company's rejection of early modern dress makes amply clear, Edward's Boys are, as Mills puts it,

> most definitely not attempting to 'explore Original Practices',
> whatever that phrase may mean. *We simply aim to put on
> a good show* using these largely unperformed and frequently
> excellent plays with an all-boy company. If, sometimes, people
> choose to think to themselves that maybe that was how it was
> done in 1588 or 1605 then perhaps the project … does offer
> occasional 'glimpses' into possibilities. ('In the Company'
> 282, emphasis added)

For Edward's Boys, that is, the guiding principle for the exploration of early modern drama through performance is one of personnel rather than properties. I would suggest, however, that the work of Edward's Boys and their 'simple' aim 'to put on a good show' do not exempt the company from the concerns of many more overtly research-based exercises into historical performance. Though the performances of Edward's Boys are not designed as research projects in their own right, their exploration through rehearsal and performance of what Stephen Purcell terms the 'here-and-now of embodied practice' arguably brings them into dialogue with the practices of the past ('Practice-as-Research' 430). 'Putting on a good show', after all, would without doubt have been the overriding concern for every early modern acting company.[21] Dani Bedau and D. J. Hopkins suggest that, since 'Shakespeare worked in contemporary performance modes', adopting

---

[21] For a strong argument in favour of student theatre's surprisingly close relation to the work of early modern acting companies, see Lopez, 'The Seeds of Time' 41.

'authentic' rather than contemporary approaches to performance is, paradoxically, 'profoundly un-Shakespearean' (152). In their use of contemporary production resources and their reliance on the tight-knit ensemble that has developed over the course of more than a decade, that is, the Boys' activities are in some ways analogous to those of their early modern forebears.

Arguing for the urgent need for more performance-based explorations – or simply more performances – of non-Shakespearean early modern drama, Richard Allen Cave makes the obvious, yet all too often overlooked, point that

> The need for sensitive 'ensemble'-style awareness in the performing of certain scenes in Shakespeare has been recognised simply because his plays have been extensively staged, and staged in accordance with allegiance to a wealth of modes and styles of acting; but this has not been readily the case with the plays of Shakespeare's contemporaries, which have tended to be relegated to an inferior status. Research through practice can help to re-evaluate the range of dramaturgical experimentation in the early decades of the seventeenth century and hopefully invite in consequence a reassessment of the skills and performance standards of the acting companies who first staged such work. ('The Value')

With the exception of Rutter's initial workshops, the activities of Edward's Boys have never been framed by specific research 'questions'. Their experimentation with modes of performing plays with virtually non-existent performance histories nevertheless places them in the role of embodied researcher. While Mills may contend that the company is not interested in 'archaeology',[22] Edward's Boys' practical work with underperformed and understudied early modern playtexts engages past performances through social embodiment in a way that is surprisingly concomitant with

---

[22] As he does in the 'Director's Ramblings' which preface the programme for the company's 2018 collaborative showcase with the choir of St Paul's Cathedral, *When Paul's Boys Met Edward's Boys.*

archaeology as practised. In their brilliant study of the overlapping disciplines of theatre and archaeology, Mike Pearson and Michael Shanks develop a model of 'interpretive archaeology' which centres on the social and processual. For them, 'interpretive archaeology' constitutes

> a set of approaches to the ruined material past which foreground interpretation, the ongoing process of making sense of what never was firm or certain. This archaeology entertains no final and definitive account of the past as it was, but fosters multivocal and multiple accounts: a creative but none the less critical attention and response to the interests, needs and desires of different constituencies (those people, groups or communities who have or express interest in the material past). (xvii)

In this light, archaeology is not a matter of digging up, just as for Edward's Boys performing early modern drama has little to with early modern artefacts (those wretched cumbersome RSC dresses). Instead, archaeology, like the performance of early modern drama today, constitutes

> a contemporary material practice which works on and with the traces of the past and within which the archaeologist is implicated as an active agent of interpretation. What archaeologists do is work with material traces, with evidence, in order to create something – a meaning, a narrative, an image – which stands for the past in the present ... Rather than being a reconstruction of the past from its surviving remains, this is a recontextualisation. (11)

In their ongoing commitment to reproducing and 'recontextualising' early modern drama in the present, Edward's Boys, like archaeologists, 'take up and make something of the past' (Pearson and Shanks 50). The sections that follow consider the means by which the company's collaborative ethos and rehearsal and performance practices 'work on and with the traces of the past' that constitute the early modern playtext, subjecting those traces to embodied processes and systems of knowledge and, in turn, producing new forms of knowledge through performance.

2 'Making the Script Work': The Actors and the Text

It is a weekday lunch time in early February 2018. I am sitting in KES's drama studio, and across the room from me, Perry Mills is gathered around the table with two boys from the Sixth Form, Joe Pocknell and Jack Hawkins. The three of them are hard at work on a scene from Lyly's The Woman in the Moon, *whose first performance is under a month away. Pocknell (the production's Pandora) and Hawkins (Gunophilus) read through act four, scene one of Lyly's play from photocopies of Leah Scragg's 2008 edition for the Revels series, which, pens always at the ready, they mark up relentlessly. Although the company has not yet finished 'blocking' the play, the forty-five-minute rehearsal is remarkably physical for a table-bound session and a far cry from the 'desperately dull' viewing experience Mills warned me it would be. As time wears on, it becomes clear that reading the lines is a secondary exercise: throughout their work on the scene, the boys routinely stop to visualise their entrances and exits, speculating on how 'sinuously and sexily' Pocknell might move across the stage at certain points, thinking about how individual actions – a well-timed slap to the face, the handing over of a prop – will cue or restrict the actions of their fellow performers. As suggestions are thrown around in quick succession, the boys and Mills reflect upon movement decisions made in earlier rehearsals, working today's physical decisions into the play as a whole. Occasionally, they test out particular sequences, getting up from the table to time how long it might take to cross the stage – a space whose dimensions will change seven times when the boys are on tour. Returning to their seats, they scribble furiously on the pages of their scripts, superimposing a series of roughly drawn oblongs, crosses, and arrows onto Lyly's words.*

What I describe here is a dominant feature of Edward's Boys' approach to performing early modern drama. Despite the table-bound nature of the session I witnessed at a relatively late stage in the 2018 rehearsal process, it is clear that the task of staging any play is not solely governed by the authorial text. This might seem a surprising claim to make in the context of the specific plays the company typically stages: for decades, early modern boy company plays have been assessed as overtly 'literary' exercises, designed for unknowing performers whose juvenility characterised them with what Bart van Es calls 'the same impressionability of print' (200). It would be naïve to dispute the obvious hierarchical structures that may indeed have provided early modern boy actors with less licence for deviation from the author's words than may have been typical in the adult companies. Nevertheless, characterising boy company drama as 'literary' to the point of being non-dramatic risks eliding its openness to physical experimentation and play, limiting our responses to it in performance today. Despite the high praise Edward's Boys routinely receive for their performances, a sense of the actors as transparent vessels through which the author's work is transmitted pervades academic reviews of their productions: Eoin Price, for instance, recalls that 'when I was watching *Galatea* it occurred to me that although the audience were very clearly and rightly appreciative of the efforts of the actors and production crew, they were also applauding Lyly' ('Monsters'). I myself recall observing an eminent Shakespeare scholar who, during a performance of the company's 2017 *Summer's Last Will and Testament*, sat 'watching' the entire thing with his eyes closed, the musicality of Nashe's prose apparently the sole focus of his attention. Indeed, this is precisely what he asked Mills – not the actors – about in the post-performance discussion session. This is an extreme (if amusing) example, but to endorse the notion that the language and applaudable craft of the author are what is at stake in an Edward's Boys performance is, I suggest, to efface the means by which the actors and their director shape and contour the authorial text to a particular set of performance circumstances and collective expertise.

This is not to suggest, however, that the authorial text is not a prominent feature of the company's rehearsal and performance processes: 'work on a play', writes erstwhile actor Alex Mills, 'starts with the text and never stops' ('What Has Edward's Boys Ever Done for Us?'). Nor is granting this prominence unreasonable given Edward's Boys' twenty-first-century school environment. Since the boys are well used to analysing and discussing a text in minute detail from their English lessons, it makes complete sense to arrive at an understanding of the text in the most pragmatic sense through these familiar learning processes. For Mills and the boys, comprehension, rather than a fetishisation of authorial intention or genius, is the principal aim: as Mills explained in a 2015 interview with Heather Neill, the company's 'endless text-bashing' ensures that 'everybody knows what they're saying' by the time it comes to 'put it on its feet' ('The Ford Experiment'). For actors like Dan Wilkinson, preparing an Edward's Boys production takes the form of 'a weird English class for the first three quarters of the "rehearsal process": you sat in a room with Perry and a couple of others, or just you, going through the text' (personal interview).[23]

For Mills, in fact, text is 'everything. It's everything for me' (personal interview, 2020). In one of our discussions after a rehearsal for the company's 2020 production of Jonson's *The Silent Woman*,[24] Mills told me that the mantra he 'lives by' when preparing a production is inspired by Trevor Nunn. In a 2018 interview, the former RSC director urges his fellow directors 'to combine as totally as humanly possible with the writer – love the writer, honour the writer, *release the writer, deliver the writer* ... the

---

[23] Wilkinson's involvement in the company spanned ten productions between 2010 and 2016: he appeared as a servant and porter in *A Chaste Maid in Cheapside* (2010); Prisius in *Mother Bombie* (2010); a member of the chorus in *Antonio's Revenge* (2011); Sergeant Clutch in *Westward Ho!* (2012); Michael Williams in *Henry V*; Dido in *Dido, Queen of Carthage*; Diana in *Galatea*; Benazzi in *The Lady's Trial*; Gondarino in *The Woman Hater*; and the Earl of Northumberland in *Will at Westminster*.

[24] I follow the company in using this title rather than the more conventional *Epicene*. One week before opening night, all performances of the production were cancelled due to the escalating Covid-19 pandemic. Given my focus on process over product throughout this Element, I feel justified in including my observations from the rehearsal period here and hope that they offer some sense of what the production might have been like. See also McCarthy, 'The One that Got Away'.

writer is the beginning and the end' (qtd. in Bowie-Sell, emphasis added). In this, Mills subscribes to a notion of performance – particularly Shakespeare performance – which pervades present-day thinking among practitioners and scholars. As W. B. Worthen has amply demonstrated, much contemporary thinking sees performance as authorised by, and subservient to, the author's text (*Authority*). Mills's description of his practice thus seems to endorse a theatrical paradigm which persists in characterising performance 'either as performance *of* the plays or as performance inscribed *in* dramatic speech – never or rarely as a formative force, as an institutionalized power in itself' (Weimann 4–5). This paradigm has recently seen RSC Artistic Director Gregory Doran advocating for a return to '*reading* and *reciting* the Bard's great works' by setting up a 'Shakespeare Gym' for authentic verse speaking (Singh, emphasis added). In this light, Edward's Boys might be characterised, as their early modern forebears have often been, as servants to the honourable, lovable (and always male) writer.

As my discussion of the *The Woman in the Moon* rehearsal suggests, however, the Edward's Boys rehearsal room text is not merely the object of straightforward transmission but a site of physical exploration and experimentation – something to be reshaped by movement. Elisabeth Dutton has identified the company's two strengths as 'painstaking attention to the text' and 'a culture in which the boys teach and learn from each other, releasing the exuberant will to perform' (qtd. in 'Expert Opinion'). In the rehearsal room, these elements productively combine, 'adapting' the text, in Robert Weimann's words, 'to materially given circumstances' (17). For the company, this process is defined by an ethos of craftsmanship and physical labour. What Rutter identified over the course of her work with the boys as 'the hard business of making the script work' is now known ubiquitously among the company as a 'job o' work' – a phrase which finds its way, consistently and insistently, into rehearsal and production documents. The boys are instructed at the first, and usually only, whole-group assembly at the beginning of the rehearsal process (known as 'The Big Meeting') that the production will primarily succeed through a 'Job o' Work' ('*Grobiana's Nuptials* – Big Meeting'). They and their parents, in letters home about the run-up to performances, are reminded that 'We have a "Job o' Work" to do' ('*The Lady's Trial* at the SWP'). By happy coincidence, the phrase 'job o[f] work' first appears in reference to the mounting of masques and interludes at the court of Edward VI, in whose name KES was founded: the Revels accounts record payments to those 'doinge certen Jobbes of woorke' (Feuillerat 236).[25] Its use in this present-day context thus unwittingly reinforces the connection between mounting an early modern performance in the sixteenth and twenty-first centuries.

To conceive of the relationship between company and text as one not of *release* and *delivery* but of *work* on and with the author's words is to accord a greater level of agency to the actors. The parallels Terry Eagleton draws between any text's production of ideology and the dramatic production's re-authoring of the text provide a fitting model here. For Eagleton, 'The relation between text and production is a relation of *labour*: the theatrical instruments (staging, acting skills and so on) transform the "raw materials" of the text into a specific product, which cannot be mechanically extrapolated from an inspection of the text itself' (65). Central to this relation, I suggest, is the intervening agency of Edward's Boys' actors, who subject the text, in Worthen's words, 'to rewriting that embodies the performative constraints and conventions of a specific mode of theatricality' (*Force* 23). *Pace* Mills's textual enthusiasm, it seems more accurate to say that rather than being 'everything', the text is instead a jumping-off point for the company-based enterprise of physical exploration and ensemble performance. The exigencies of such a performance mode are detectable even in the 'weird English classes' which dominate the initial phases of the rehearsal process.

What happens, then, to the text in its remaking in performance? Given the lesson-like quality attributed to the majority of the company's rehearsal process one might expect a great deal of emphasis to be placed on verse speaking, pronunciation, and instruction in metrical delivery. Doran, in his rallying cry for a 'Shakespeare Gym', describes such activities as 'workouts' which ensure 'that everybody has the iambic pentameter in their bloodstream' (qtd. in Singh). Mills's prompt copies of the scripts, however, preserve little evidence of such activity. Occasionally, a particular speech's rhetorical dynamics do seem to have been teased out, particularly when they have the potential to be overemphasised in performance for comic effect. One such passage is a speech given by the 'lascivious smell-feast' Lazarillo in *The*

[25] See also *OED*, 'job, n. 2, P1'.

Woman Hater, who struggles to contain his rage after discovering that a rare and much-coveted fish head has gone missing. Mills's copy of the script, based on Fredson Bowers's edition of the play, zeroes in on the rhetorical device of isocolon which ironises Lazarillo's distress:

> I will <u>not</u> curse, <u>nor</u> swear, <u>nor</u> rage, <u>nor</u> rail,
> <u>Nor</u> with contemptuous tongue accuse my fate
> (Though I might justly do it;) <u>nor</u> will I
> Wish myself uncreated, for this evil!

(2.1.348–51; p. 24)

What is less clear is the extent to which Mills and the company regard such textual features as *instructions* for delivery. In the recorded 2016 performance of *The Woman Hater*, Dan Powers's Lazarillo did not place particular emphasis on the repeated 'nors', suggesting that the speaking of the words was ultimately left up to him even if attention had been paid to these rhetorical features in earlier rehearsals. Indeed, Mills insists that vocal delivery is not the focus of the company's 'endless text-bashing'. 'It's very rare', he explains, 'that I'll say, "they pronounced e-r-e as 'ere'" – that's not what's important. It's us talking about it' (personal interview, 2018). The ultimate aim is total immersion in the text. The focus of this immersion is not rhetorical delivery – the instructions for which, as work such as Abigail Rokison's reminds us, are arguably contained within the text itself – but of ownership: 'Throughout this "process" we talk about everything – what the words say and what they might mean . . . We interrogate every line, every word, even the silences. Even the filthy jokes . . . [T]he aim is for the boys to take over the language, *possess it as their own*' (Mills, 'In the Company' 276, emphasis added).

   I do not mean to suggest that this approach is unique to Edward's Boys. Given the unfamiliarity of early modern drama even to professionally trained actors, table work such as I describe here is a widespread feature of contemporary theatrical practice. What I wish to stress, however, is the particular importance of this approach in Edward's Boys' educational context. In insisting on 'talking about everything', Mills harnesses familiar pedagogical methods from elsewhere in the boys' school life to enhance their engagement with the text. A crucial dimension of this activity is that these sessions are almost always isolated occasions, carried out with a very small number of the company's actors at any one time. Again, the company's educational context is a deciding factor. From its scrappy documentation in the company's archive, this stage in a production's development seems to be considerably ad hoc. As Mills explained to me in an email,

> My rehearsal process was once described by a colleague as 'rehearsing under the cover of darkness'. I like it to be low-key. I generally begin for a March production in late November/early December. Our great advantage, being in an institution like a school, is TIME so we rehearse little and often over the next weeks and months. We are all busy people so I tend to rehearse mainly with very small groups and fit round their other commitments. Consequently, the only person to attend everything is me. ('Re: Edward's Boys')

The school environment and the teacher–pupil relationships, that is, can be capitalised upon in the service of the authorial text, the comprehension of which is essential to performance.

In rehearsals I have observed, even the youngest members of the company, who may not have any lines at all in the given scene, are required to become intensely familiar with any part of the play in which they appear. The advantages of this approach were made apparent to me in a one-on-one text-bashing session I observed during the short 2018 rehearsal period for *When Paul's Boys Met Edward's Boys*, a unique collaboration between the company and the choristers of St Paul's Cathedral. The session was devoted to instructing thirteen-year-old Jyan Dutton, who had been cast as Castilio in act three, scene one of *Antonio's Revenge* and the servant in act three, scene three of *A Chaste Maid in Cheapside*. Though Dutton had no lines in the former scene and only one in the latter, in the half-hour rehearsal the scenes were read aloud in their entirety, with Mills stopping frequently to convey a sense of each character's key traits or provide a gloss on specific phrases and the overall tone of the plays ('*Chaste Maid* is a very bawdy comedy. That means it's about sex'). This rehearsal-cum-English-lesson therefore functioned as more than instruction in delivering the lines: it was also an immersion in the play as a whole.

Actors have remarked that, as well as enhancing linguistic competence, Mills's frequent glossing making the unfamiliar familiar, these rehearsals allow them to get under the skin of the playtext – quite literally when it comes to those 'bawdy comedies'. This often leads to the actors having a deeper understanding of their individual characters. Recalling his performance as Gondarino, *The Woman Hater*'s titular misogynist, Wilkinson remarks that

> we had no clue what the hell was going on. We'd got it by the end, though. It worked. At the start I thought, 'am I just a rampant misogynist?' But actually no, that's not what's going on, there's a million layers to it . . . We realised that I wasn't an old, weird man; I was actually really sexually repressed. (personal interview)

Minute textual work, that is, ultimately enhanced Wilkinson's psychological understanding, and thus portrayal, of the role.

So far, so modern, so Stanislavskian. Such an intensive text-based approach seems, at first blush, to have little correspondence to what we (think we) know about early modern rehearsal practices. As Tiffany Stern has influentially demonstrated, the demands of the early modern repertory system and the part-based approach to line learning were such that little time appears to have been left for introspective characterisation or, indeed, familiarity with the play (10–12). Rehearsals do, however, appear to have taken place, at least occasionally, 'in the presence of an "instructor" . . . who helped further to prescribe the rules that limited verbal and gestural range' (11) – a dynamic not dissimilar from that on display in the 'text-bashing' sessions that take place every lunchtime in KES's Memorial Library.[26]

---

[26] John Rice, for instance, received paid-for private instruction from the veteran actor John Heminges in preparation for delivering 'a short speech containing eighteen verses, devised by Master Ben Jonson the poet' before King James in 1607 (see Kathman 248–9). Evelyn Tribble has recently modified Stern's

The Edward's Boys early rehearsal process may, then, partially bridge the temporal gap between seventeenth- and twenty-first-century practices.

Interestingly enough, in Stern's later work with Simon Palfrey, the authors suggest that the early modern rehearsal system 'highlights the centrality of individual actors, owning the parts they played', whereby 'the whole tone and manner of the character were . . . determined in isolation' (4, 62). As Wilkinson's comments suggest, determination of tone and manner is also the product of isolated preparation for Edward's Boys. Given that many of the texts with which the boys work are unfamiliar and largely unedited, working through a photocopied text devoid of scholarly apparatus forces the boys to collaborate in the mutual creation of meaning. Actors have repeatedly remarked on the familiarity and advantages of this process. In a series of interviews filmed in 2015, Wilkinson remarks that 'having a small part and coming in two or three weeks before it [the production] opened' no longer feels 'alien'. His colleague, Fin Hatch, paradoxically suggests that keeping actors separate until the final stages actually 'helps with forming a company' since it avoids smaller roles sitting in whole-group rehearsals thinking 'this play hasn't got anything to do with me; why am I here, what's the point?' (*Film Extracts*). The individualised approach to understanding and rehearsing the text thus creates a sense of part-ownership in which each actor develops a sense of what Mills has described to the boys as 'the "journey" your character takes throughout the performance, how s/he contributes to the whole piece' ('Sunday 8th March'). Wilkinson and Hatch's endorsement of this process demonstrates the extent to which the approach develops the boys' confidence and autonomy in performance.

Elsewhere in my rehearsal observations, it has been clear how readily the more experienced players of the company have adapted to this approach. During an early rehearsal for *The Silent Woman*, actors Ewan Craig and Felix Kerrison-Adams (Clerimont and Dauphine Eugenie respectively) demonstrated a well-honed aptitude for identifying linguistic patterns, stylistic features which suggest particular modes of delivery, and significant recurring motifs which contributed to the actors' sense of the play and their

staunchly individualistic model of rehearsal, plausibly suggesting 'the possibility that actors worked together in smaller, more *ad hoc* groups' (*Cognition* 66).

role within it.[27] As they read through and discussed the play's opening scene, the boys often stopped unprompted to discuss the chatty prosaic nature of the gallant's dialogue, with Craig suggesting that the two characters' witty repartee ought to be delivered at a clattering pace. It was clear in this rehearsal that these two experienced actors had harnessed lessons learned in previous productions which allowed them to transform the author's text into their own long before the time came to put it on its feet. For experienced actors of the company, familiarity with the processes of text-bashing can allow them to take ownership of even the most daunting of speeches. Without this kind of preparation, feats such as George Ellingham's animate delivery of a twelve-minute speech as Winter in Nashe's *Summer's Last Will and Testament* (2017) simply would not have been possible (see McCarthy, 'Review of *Summer's Last Will*').

Despite the apparent emphasis on linguistic clarity and character developments in these small-group text tutorials, a focus on corporeality is also discernible. For the company, text work is not primarily a mode of psychological exploration: it is first and foremost a case of seeking physical opportunities. Throughout the rehearsal with Dutton, for instance, Mills often paused to depict how he saw the scene coming together onstage. In *Chaste Maid*, Dutton himself would, Mills suggested, spring onto the stage to deliver the line 'Your white mare's ready' (3.3.142) and 'hit it big and loud'. As Mills recently explained to me in an email, 'Much of the releasing of the potential for movement happens as we sit around the table ... The ideas tumble out continually in almost every rehearsal. We are always saying things like, "It sounds like they are close together ... far apart ... one behind the other ... turning in the doorway"' ('Re: Rehearsals'). This is not to say that in their work around the table Mills and the boys are constantly on the lookout for the 'field of perceptual and corporeal activity that exists as a latency within the text' argued for by performance phenomenologists such as Stanton B. Garner, Jr. (7). Rather, what emerges from examining multiple company scripts is a sense that the company is consistently alert to where bodies might *intervene*, whether or not the text seems

---

[27] By this point, Craig had appeared in five productions since 2017, Kerrison-Adams in seven.

specifically to demand such intervention. The scripts of Edward's Boys actors are, in Barbara Hodgdon's formulation, '*embodied* books – proxies that trace voice and body, relations between bodies and theatrical time and timing' (*Shakespeare, Performance and the Archive* 42).

Work on the 2011 production of *Antonio's Revenge* seems to have been particularly geared to the text's minute physical realisation: Mills's prompt script is laden with underlines which often directly correspond to stage action. His rendering of the climactic murder of Julio in act three, scene one reads, '<u>thus</u>, <u>thus</u>, / And <u>thus</u> I'll punch it', each thus, in the filmed production, becoming violent mimed stabs to the young boy's torso, accompanied by the offstage sound effect of slashing knives. The boys, too, are taught to identify the blocking potential that is inherent to the printed text. A script belonging to the production's Nutriche (Henry Edwards) is similarly marked with physical pointers. His opening speech, for instance, is annotated as follows:[28]

> Marry, you have disturbed the pleasure of the finest dream.
> O God! I was even <u>coming</u> to it, la. O Jesu! 'twas <u>coming</u> of
> the sweetest. I'll tell you now, methought I was married, and
> methought I <u>spent</u> (O lord, why did you wake me?) and
> methought I <u>spent</u> three <u>spur-royals</u> on the <u>fiddlers</u> for
> striking up a <u>fresh hornpipe</u>. (1.2.31–8)

Allowing no innuendo to go to waste, in performance Edwards mapped these annotations onto his vocal inflection and physicality, placing particular stresses on the highlighted words and accompanying each with an over-emphasised gesture – a knowing look or wink, or collusively pointing a finger, eyebrows raised, at a member of the audience to accentuate the pun. Edwards recalls how frequently the mapping of movement onto text

---

[28] Edwards performed in three other productions besides *Antonio's Revenge*: as Mistress Touchwood in *A Chaste Maid in Cheapside*, Christian in *Westward Ho!*, and the Bishop of Ely in *Henry V*. For ease of reading, I have replaced the thick red circles Edwards has drawn around the words in this passage with underlining. I am grateful to Edwards for donating his Edward's Boys scripts to me.

formed part of even the earliest rehearsals – a process which proved particularly beneficial to his role as the Bishop of Ely in *Henry V* (personal interview). Here, Ely and Canterbury's (Henry Hodson) recounting of Henry's claim to the French throne through recourse to Salic law was rendered visually through the use of a blackboard: having been thrown a piece of chalk at the outset of the speech, Edwards punctuated the notoriously long speech by drawing frenzied diagrams, his writing becoming increasingly small and cramped until, at the speech's conclusion, he drew a long, triumphant line linking the genealogical strands together, prompting laughter and applause. The physical realisation of this speech required particularly close attention: Edwards's script has the twelve names who make up the complex web of genealogical association highlighted, and he recalls an entire rehearsal spent 'just sitting at a table discussing Salic law and how it all worked and what Henry [Hodson] was saying so that I could make it happen visually to make the audience understand it' (personal interview). Time and again in the material traces and actors' recollections of the rehearsal process, we find close textual study corresponding directly to movement. In Edwards's performances, the 'bashed' text is remade through performance behaviours – revelry in salacious audacity or boyish physicality – which befit the company's production style.

During these rehearsals, the company frequently engages in acts of representing the text in spatial terms. For any given production, the scripts used by Mills and the boys are covered with sketches of the stage space, within which the movements of characters are represented by arrows. Many of these are created while the actors are still seated around that omnipresent table. The long act two, scene one of *The Woman Hater*, for instance, is in Mills's script represented by a series of such diagrams which enabled him and the actors to answer the question scribbled on the back of one of the pages: 'How do they all interact?' In the scene in question, a number of characters – the Duke and his associates Arrigo and Lucio; the Count Valore, his sister Oriana, and her waiting woman; the smell-feast Lazarillo and his serving boy – pass through Gondarino's house and interact in various groupings, overhearing one another and remarking in aside on the actions of another group. Though there are no directions for any such movement in Beaumont's text, in the hands of Edward's Boys the scene became an exercise in crossed

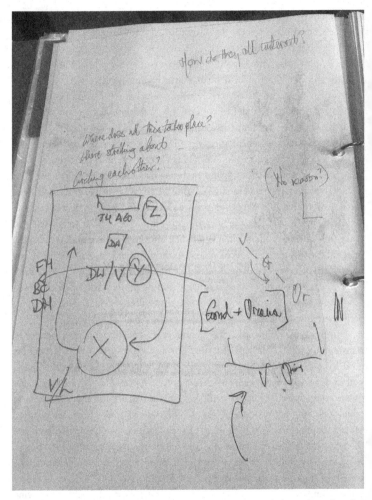

Figure 4 A sample page from Perry Mills's copy of the script for the company's 2016 production of Francis Beaumont's *The Woman Hater*. Photo by Harry R. McCarthy, reproduced with permission.

paths and continuous circling, as shown in Figure 4. In preparing this scene for performance, the company envisaged Gondarino's sense of continual invasion and the other characters' criss-crossing observations and interactions as a series of shifting spatial configurations rather than mere dialogic 'delivery'. What becomes important here, as so often in Edward's Boys' rehearsals and productions, is not the words of the text but the movements of the performers, a replacement of 'author's pen' not, as Weimann would have it, with 'actor's voice' but with actor's *body*.

Time and again in their table-bound rehearsals, Edward's Boys impose a robust physicality onto the text which extends beyond seeking deictic instruction from the author's words. As Felix Crabtree remarked of his performance as Iphicles in the company's *The Woman in the Moon*, much of the company's physical humour is 'not in the text, though you can infer it from the text. It's not plainly there written' (qtd. in Davies). The actors' sense of physicality as an intervening force chimes with Worthen's assertion that '[s]tage production does more than merely evoke, enunciate, or complete the text; it re-presents the text in a variety of incommensurable visual, embodied, kinetic discourses' (*Authority* 62). For all the omnipresence of tables and folders in the rehearsal room, the interaction between text and performance is truly a bilateral process for the company rather than a question of unidirectional transmission. Throughout their early rehearsals, Edward's Boys harness their educational environment and carefully honed skills of textual interpretation to find ways of bringing their skill sets and systems of behaviour to bear on the text. Imposing dynamics that lie outside the text onto its stage articulation, Edward's Boys help to expand our sense of what the 'play' actually is.

3 The Text on Its Feet: Encountering the Past, Embodying the Present

For Edward's Boys, the text work described in the previous section is essential to developing a physical feel for the play in performance. Several of the actors remark that getting the text 'up on its feet' is a relatively swift process, which many of them see as a direct result of that early textual work. Even in the earliest years of the company's formation, young actor Oliver Hayes stated that 'The process of putting a play on its feet, once the text has been studied to a high enough standard, is rather a quick one' ('CAPITAL').[29] Mills has more recently suggested that a two-and-a-half-hour show tends to be blocked in just six days – a process which is 'quite "boom-boom-boom"' (personal interview, 2018). The correlation Hayes identifies between textual work and blocking is instructive, and several of the boys have expressed a preference for this way of working. When asked in an interview if he would prefer to get the text up on its feet earlier than has become typical, Joe Pocknell asserts that 'The longer we leave it, the better we understand it, and so the blocking becomes easier – it becomes more natural because you know why you're doing it'. In the same interview, Dan Wilkinson describes how, in the wake of close textual work, 'the blocking just writes itself' (*Film Extracts*). More recently, having left the company after performing in ten productions, Wilkinson has elaborated on this observation, explaining that 'the play just kind of happens, because *the text is so ridiculously instructive*' (personal interview, emphasis added).

The company's early textual exploration, that is, places the boys in a secure position to 'own' the playwright's words through embodied processes. As the previous section has shown, even the most text-based of enterprises functions as a physical and pragmatic exploration of an early modern playtext, despite individual actors' considerations of their characters' psychology. For Christian Billing, the emphasis on psychological exploration in performing early modern drama has

> stood as a significant blocking device militating against the innovative preparation and performance of the text. Specifically, it is a principle that has prohibited: (i) useful exploration of a range of more thoroughly-historicized approaches to actor-training and rehearsal processes; (ii) wider theatre-anthropological understandings of rehearsal

---

[29] Here, Hayes is recalling his performances as Freevill in *Dutch Courtesan*, Sir Bounteous Progress in *A Mad World, My Masters*, and Sir Walter Whorehound in *Chaste Maid*.

and performance; and (iii) consideration of what may also usefully be employed from more wide-ranging research and practice, including techniques derived from the theatrical genres of ensemble and devising practices. (402–3)

The Edward's Boys rehearsal studio, I suggest, permits a departure from the kind of stifling activity Billing decries. Instead, it permits understanding of the processes by which an early modern play comes to be performed through a more anthropological, ensemble-based, and even historicised lens. Examining a theatre company in rehearsal, Gay McAuley argues, ought to be 'a central element in the academic study of performance' for this very reason. Such a study, she suggests, engages the possibility of turning away from 'concern with the individual work of art' and towards 'the social and cultural context within which that work is being created' (2, 5). Billing describes such activity as the *only* means of accessing the 'essence' of the early modern playtext: 'until we get into the rehearsal room and expose Shakespeare (or any other printed play-text) to the active and embodied processes of collaborative investigation, risk, play and the repeated creating of exploratory interpretations that constitute rehearsal practice ...[,] we have none of us cracked the spine' of any of Shakespeare's plays and, accordingly, that we none of us actually have the vaguest idea what any of these texts contain' (384).

Billing's emphasis on the agential force of rehearsal is refreshing, though it must be said that to ascribe 'containment' to the playtext continues to promote a unidirectional sense of textual authority and its transmission in performance. Indeed, as Billing goes on to suggest, 'The Shakespearean text itself contains no truths, no answers; and in a very real sense, it does not exist at all until it is moving and breathing; living through ... engaged and appropriately deployed bodies of knowledge' (387). It is these engaged and appropriately deployed bodies of knowledge that interest me here. I suggest that, when we watch Edward's Boys 'putting a play on its feet', we can better understand the plays on which they work. I mean this not only in the sense that they may partially capture the frisson and excitement of watching these plays in performance by boys (and, as reviewers often comment, they undeniably *do* do that). The oft-touted mantra of 'process over product' becomes particularly important in the case of the plays that Edward's Boys perform given the slightness of their performance histories. In some cases, Edward's Boys are the first practitioners to work, moment by moment, through these plays since their original performers. Their rehearsals thus become a powerful site of historical re-encounter – arguably more so than is the case for the plays of Shakespeare. Barbara Hodgdon argues of Shakespearean rehearsal that 'recuperating some features of [a] production's rehearsal life' can contribute 'not only to our understanding of the playtext but also by what we mean by "the play"' ('Rehearsal Process' 11). While I do not suggest that Edward's Boys' way of rehearsing and performing these plays is the *only* way, their ensemble experience of doing so allows us to think more carefully than has previously been possible about the embodied processes involved in their staging.

For Rob Conkie, 'rehearsal primarily exceeds performance via its repetitions and variations as an interpretive mode: rehearsal, of course, is the practical means of interpreting the text' ('Rehearsal' 424–5). As I demonstrated in the previous section, much of the textual interpretation carried out by Edward's Boys is concerned with giving a physical shape to any given play, under- and overlaying its words with corporeal motion. In the rehearsal studio, much of the 'boom-boom-boom' blocking process concentrates on who exactly is required to move, where to, and when – a re-embodiment of the already-embodied diagrammatic thinking so evident in the scribbles and scrawls on the pages of their scripts. The blocking process for the company's 2020 production of *The Silent Woman* necessitated a particular engagement with this kind of thinking. One of the rehearsals I attended, which had the nominal aim of 'running' the whole of the production's second half, instead became entirely consumed with working through the movements across the stage which seem to be required of a large number of actors in act three, scenes four through six.[30] During this sequence, Morose (Nilay Sah) converses with the barber Cutbeard (Ricky Cooke) and the parson (Rhys Duncan) before rudely dismissing them. To Morose's horror, his new wife, Epicene (Will Groves), begins to

[30] I follow the company in adopting David Bevington's scene designations in the 2012 Cambridge edition of Jonson's works.

chastise him, and his torment is compounded with the arrival of Truewit (Ritvick Nagar) who begins to taunt him, followed by the foolish Sir John Daw (Jamie Mitchell) and the fearsome Ladies Collegiate (Enrique Burchill, Tom Howitt, Callum Maughan, and Seb Steven). Morose makes to leave but is detained by Truewit and, observed by Truewit and Morose, Daw introduces the ladies to Epicene. Away from Morose's earshot, Truewit joins the ladies and conspires with them and, eventually, they bring Morose into the discussion against his will. The busyness of the scene, even on the page, is obvious. Yet the page alone cannot clarify the ways in which the sequence routinely shifts focus, requiring groupings of actors to come together and separate, avoiding one another at crucial moments yet nevertheless moving around when their lines of dialogue explicitly invite it. A sense of the complex spatial negotiation the scene demands of its actors moving through space is captured in my rehearsal diary from the blocking session:[31]

> *Earlier in the scene, Morose has ended up downstage left (DSL). Now, when the Ladies Collegiate arrive from upstage right (USR; the entrance designated by the company as leading from a separate room in the house) and move towards Epicene, they quickly end up behind Morose and make his avoidance of them difficult. The company agrees that Morose will therefore need to have cleared the downstage space earlier in the scene, moving right across the stage so that he is face-to-face with John Daw in time to address him. Truewit will need to track these movements closely, ensuring*

---

[31] The production was destined to tour to multiple venues, including Durham Cathedral, the King's Hall at Newcastle University, Riddle's Court in Edinburgh, the Workshop Theatre at Leeds University, and the Sam Wanamaker Playhouse. To facilitate ease of adapting between venues, the production design was therefore sparse, consisting of two doors at the back of the stage with a large screen (over the top of which the actors could occasionally peer) in the middle. No furniture was to be used throughout the production.

that he is able to move between Morose and the Ladies as the
lines demand.

As we work through the scene, we hit upon sticking point
after sticking point: the introduction of each new character or
group of characters brings them into unhelpful collision with
those already on stage, sometimes in direct contradiction of
the words on the page – Morose, for instance, cannot come
into contact with the Ladies Collegiate when he is explicitly
trying to avoid them. As yet another of these sticking points
arises, Mills remarks, 'It's like we're chasing a hare or
something: every time we get to the next bit, everything else
needs changing'.

We work backwards through the text: where are the focal
points? Nagar suggests that at present the Ladies are forming an
unhelpful barrier: they need to move over to one side to allow for
Morose's attempts to escape. Perhaps Daw could bring them
DSR to meet Epicene, rather than moving her upstage to meet
them? This clears a space: later in the scene, the Ladies can
retreat further upstage, allowing Daw to move back downstage
and come face to face with Morose just as Morose says, referring
to Daw, 'What is this?' These positions free up the front of the
stage for Morose to move back across it, only to be stalled by
Truewit who hauls him back upstage to introduce him to the
Ladies. Having, finally, worked this sequence out, Mills returns
*to his seat exclaiming, '*This *one doesn't block its bloody self!'*

Here, the boys come face to face with the need to move instinctively,
responding to the movements of other characters in the space and creating
groupings and spatial demarcations which are not written into Jonson's text.
Blocking, of course, is widespread practice in the contemporary theatre;
however, Edwards' Boys' work on a play as rarely performed as *The Silent
Woman* alerts us more readily to the play's moment-by-moment physical
exigencies. This is not a 'discovery' in the sense of having dug up a blocking
pattern latent in the script – to describe it as such would be to subscribe to
the kind of empiric certainty of which early modern scholars such as Paul

Menzer have grown suspicious (see Menzer, Afterword). Yet it is arguably an *encounter*, a recognition that the text demands that *something* needs to happen and the implementation of collective expertise to initiate it. Such encounters do not, fairly obviously, provide zero-sum interpretive clarity or confirm that Jonson did indeed require his actors to move downstage left at line 37. Rather, they help us to access the processes and decision-making required to go to work on the text of his play. Gilli Bush-Bailey and Jacky Bratton describe this encounter as 'revival', a process which 'acknowledges the present and works to reawaken that which can be brought into use again' (qtd. in Davis et al. 96, 107). In bringing Jonson's physical opportunities back into use in 2020, Edward's Boys provide valuable insight into the extratextual agency to which this process gives rise.

This stage in the company's rehearsal process also routinely opens the playtext up to opportunities for extratextual business which, on occasion, seem to be invited by the text itself. Blocking rehearsals for the company's production of *The Woman in the Moon* offered considerable scope to explore what Mills termed the 'physical punctuation' that seems to underscore Lyly's play at key moments. During a rehearsal concerned with putting act three, scene two of the play on its feet, much was made of physically exploring the alternating pace of the scene. During this scene, Pandora (Joe Pocknell) simultaneously dupes her four shepherd suitors (Felix Crabtree, Ritvick Nagar, Pascal Vogiaridis, and Charlie Waters) as well as her servant, Gunophilus (Jack Hawkins), all while smoothly playing the role of benevolent hostess. It is therefore unsurprising that Mills's annotations included the emboldened 'PACE – CONFUSION – FARCE', and it seems that he took his cue from the play's most recent editor's suggestion in private correspondence that, 'The key to the whole thing, to my mind, is pace' (Scragg, Letter). The six boys and their director approached the scene with methodical physicality. The company introduced glasses and tableware, which they used emphatically throughout the scene to enhance the lines being spoken – the rivalrous shepherds frequently slamming down a glass or suggestively pointing bananas at one another. This move picked up directly on the suggestion in the same editor's letter of 'lots of stage business (raising of glasses, reaching for fruit, people glancing from one to another, moving around the table)' in negotiating 'the seemingly hectic succession of asides'.

In rehearsal and the subsequent performance, inflecting the densely written scene's single lines of overlapping dialogue with moments of pause and stillness paradoxically served further to unlock its comic potential in the most unexpected of places. A particularly memorable moment came in response to the awkward caesura in the following exchange of lines among the shepherds:

> MELOS
>
> But ere I slept —
>
> LEARCHUS
>
>   When I had list —
>
> IPHICLES
>
>   What then?
>
> MELOS
>
> *Cetera quis nescit?*
>
>   (4.1.27–8)

Identifying two missing feet (after '*Cetera quis nescit*') in an otherwise pentametric exchange, Mills and the boys experimented with filling the four-syllable gap with an anguished, orgasmic sigh that punctuated the swelling interchange of lines. This sigh provided a direct answer to Melos's Latinised 'Who knows not the rest?' and worked as a comically visual and aural cue to the following:

> LEARCHUS
>
> Melos prevents me that I should have said.
>
> IPHICLES
>
> Blush, Iphicles, and in thy rosy cheeks
> Let all the heat that feeds thy heart appear!
>
>   (4.1.29–31)

Having already intertwined their arms and legs more closely on each spoken half-line – an imitation of a postcard of Antonio Canova's *The Three Graces*, passed around the rehearsal room – the four boys were brought by the four-syllable sigh into close physical and vocal synchronisation with one another, responding to the inherent cue of Lyly's text through syncopated

movement and exhalation (Figure 5). By the time the play reached performance, this pause had grown in orgasmic intensity – much to the delight
(and discernible shock) of the audience.

This moment in rehearsal was a firm reification of Billing's suggestion that

> both the diachronic building of character and the synchronic
> development of movements in individual scenes … often
> arise from unexpected moments of shared insight – in the
> form of one individual's response to or interpretation of
> a rehearsal text with another, or others. (384)

Here, Edward's Boys' collaborative way of working exerted upon Lyly's
playtext a corporeally engaged practice which extended beyond mere

Figure 5 Adam Hardy as Jupiter, Pascal Vogiaridis as Melos, Felix Crabtree
as Iphicles, Charlie Waters as Learchus, and Ritvick Nagar as Stesias in the
2018 production of John Lyly's *The Woman in the Moon*, directed by Perry
Mills. Photo by Lauren Hyslop, courtesy of Edward's Boys.

'delivery'. The company in rehearsal consistently negotiates with the materials of the past to create performance opportunities in the present, working together closely with the text and making pragmatic decisions relating to spatial negotiation or identifying rhythmic dynamics that open themselves up to physical play. While such rehearsals are obviously not preoccupied with 'recovering' the 'original' practices of the boy companies who performed these plays in the late sixteenth and early seventeenth centuries, I suggest that they nevertheless participate in what Rebecca Schneider powerfully describes as 'the syncopated time of re-enactment, where *then* and *now* punctuate each other' (2). When, in rehearsal, Edward's Boys come face to face with textual opportunities for physical action – less prompted by the text than invited in its interstices – they participate in a form of 'gestic negotiation' in which the text of the past is 'replay[ed] . . . back across the body' (Schneider 9). Though we cannot know whether Jonson's, or Lyly's, or anyone else's boy actors seized upon such opportunities in anything approaching a similar way, Edward's Boys' encounters with the texts of the past through the theatrical activity of the present can help us better to understand the kinds of performance behaviour to which the early modern playtext opens itself.

The studio rehearsals of Edward's Boys are not, however, merely dedicated to blocking or moving line by line through the author's text and recognising corporeal demands and opportunities. They also prioritise feeling organically through and around the play through the performing body. The best kind of Shakespeare rehearsal, Billing suggests, 'frequently *departs from text in order to return to it* – because often the most valuable insights about textual meaning, those with the greatest performative authority, are derived from *tangential approaches to the text* rather than repeated vocal iterations (or acting in response to modernized glosses) of it' (392, emphases added). Since the 2012 production of *Westward Ho!*, the company has overtly pursued such a tangential approach to rehearsing an early modern play. Central to this evolving approach to rehearsal and performance is the employment at various stages in the production process of Struan Leslie. Leslie was the founding Movement Director for the RSC and, outside of this work, is perhaps best known for his frequent collaborations with the British theatre director Katie Mitchell. Edward's Boys are highly unusual among amateur companies in their privileged access to a figure as influential as Leslie, who has directed, choreographed, and consulted on major theatrical, musical, and corporate projects across the world.[32] Though Leslie is adamant that he works with Edward's Boys 'as I work with any actor' (personal interview), the age of the boys and their physical capacities have a particular bearing on their rehearsals and performances.

On his website, Leslie defines 'the principles of choric and ensemble work' as central to his practice. These principles, he states, combine with related disciplines such as music and the visual arts to 'create work that is specific, in both devised work and in response to the extant repertoire' ('Struan's Work'). That word, 'response', is worth dwelling on in relation to Leslie's work with Edward's Boys. Typically taking the form of a handful of long movement rehearsals interspersed throughout the months leading up to the performance,[33] this work is focused not around identifying specific movements the authorial text seems to 'demand' and teaching the boys how to enact them but around creating what Leslie elsewhere terms a 'physical text' which provides the basis from which the author's words can be explored ('On Movement-Based Theatre').

For Leslie, movement-based theatre is concerned not with seeking out physical prompts in the text itself but with identifying a contained range of possibilities through which the actors can explore characterisation and the world of the play through a shared 'physical language':

> We'll refine the parameters in which the production can exist. So if you imagine that we start rehearsing the play in a huge field, and over the process of the rehearsals we start bringing in some fences, and we bring those fences closer together until we're in a nice little shape in the middle of the field … And in that process then we clarify the physical language, or the physical behaviour. So it becomes a field for improvisation, instead of it just kind of being 'right get into

---

[32] For an overview of Leslie's career, see Evans 24–30; Leslie, 'Struan's Work'.

[33] The rehearsals for *The Silent Woman*, spanning November 2019 to March 2020, included four 4-hour sessions with Leslie.

that field and move and run around,' actually no, we're working within *these* parameters ... we can just be clearer then about what that physical language is.

...

When I'm looking at a play I'm always looking at where the spaces are, what the world is, what the situation is. And then try to work with the actors to realise that in their bodies. ('On Movement-based Theatre')

Though, as I have witnessed, Leslie approaches his rehearsals with Edward's Boys with the same professionalism and rigour one would expect at, for instance, the RSC, his work remains attuned to the actors' youthful physicality. From the start, Leslie states, 'There was something about tapping into that energy of the boys and focusing it physically ... They're always filtered through being boys, and for me that's as much physical [as intellectual] ... they don't separate the physical from the intellectual ... There's not the same divide [as with adult actors]' (personal interview).

In his work with Edward's Boys, Leslie often departs from the text altogether, and tables and annotated folders are, at last, pushed aside. During one such rehearsal I observed midway through the preparations for *The Silent Woman*, Leslie conducted a lengthy exercise designed to establish the 'heightened physicality' of the playworld (the production was set in the New Romantic–obsessed world of 1980s London) while additionally developing the company's ensemble approach to performing the play. The physical immediacy of the exercise, and the remarkable effects it had on some company members' understanding of Jonson's text, is best captured by reproducing another extract from my rehearsal diary:

> *After lunch, we move from choreographing the production's final dance number to developing corporeal communication between company members. Leslie has the boys stand in a circle and move in alternate directions from person to person, grasping hands with one another, locking eyes, twisting away from one another, and moving on to the next person in the circle. A rhythm is introduced: each partnership stays in place for two beats, and, as*

the boys move from one partner to the next, there is a discernible bodily tension between the performers. Leslie remarks that these movements create the visual effect of contrapposto *– of bodies twisted in motion as they react instinctively to one another.*

Next, Leslie instructs the boys to think about their individual characters in the play and to take them *around the room on the same journey: the look they give each person and the way in which their body eventually twists away from them should be in keeping with the characters as they understand them. As the boys move, Leslie asks them to think about particular body parts with which their characters might be identified: do any of them refer to or use particular parts of their bodies? Might the servants, so used to fetching and carrying, have a particular identification with their hands? The noise-hating Morose with his ears? The painfully verbose Sir Amorous La Foole and Sir John Daw with their mouths? Having each identified a limb, organ, or (in at least one case) member, the boys move under Leslie's instruction as though guided solely by this part of the body.*

We dispense with the circle, and the boys are free to roam around the room, still guided by their defining body part. At regular intervals, the boys are instructed to change direction, ensuring that the guiding part of the body is 're-invested' and pushed out first. As the boys, instructed by Leslie, speed up, discernible characters begin to emerge, particularly when Leslie asks the boys to think about what each part of the body might sound like. The boys map their movements onto their particular lines, and I notice that several of them are coming to understand them corporeally: Ritvick Nagar's Truewit, his 'guiding body part' having been identified as his heart, starts to deliver his prose speeches in a heartbeat iamb.

I am particularly struck by how this more free-flowing motion demands that the actors closely track one another's movements: their direction of travel is determined by the presence of their fellow performers. The boys' movement around the space turns into a game: who can get into the

available space fast enough? A nonverbal mutual understanding
of the shaping of space through movement emerges here, the
combative body-based ownership of the space turning into an
exercise in collective physical understanding of the characters,
the playworld, and the performance.

In this rehearsal, movement was less about 'enlivening' the words of the play through gesture and instead focused on the creation of a physical ensemble, developing a shared corporeal vocabulary in response to the play as the actors physically understood it. When I interviewed several of the production's leads immediately after the rehearsal, they confirmed my sense that detaching movement from the specific words of the authorial text helps to develop physical ownership over the production. For Nilay Sah,[34] the production's Morose, such exercises facilitated an intense corporeal understanding of his character that extended far beyond the words on the page:

> There's no specific scene assigned to the work you're doing,
> but you really have to focus more on 'what is my character?
> How would it move?' And the fact that there's a completely
> different character, that you're not in the same scene with,
> makes you really existentially consider how they would
> react in this completely unknown, detached scenario. It
> really takes you and the characterisation back down to its
> core. (personal interview)

Exercises in 'detached', albeit characterised, motion thus develop a system of performance behaviour that extends well beyond the transmission of words. It is not for nothing that one of the names frequently invoked during

---

[34] Since 2016, Sah has appeared in five of the company's productions besides *The Silent Woman*: as Viola in *Unperfect Actors*; Ginny Lucre in *A Trick to Catch the Old One*; Back-Winter in *Summer's Last Will and Testament*; Julia from Jonson's *Poetaster* in *When Paul's Boys Met Edward's Boys*; and Instruction, Strength, and Riches in *Wit and Science*.

Leslie's work with Edward's Boys is that of Jacques Lecoq, whose physicalised approaches to rehearsal and performance Darren Tunstall has recently argued could be of serious benefit to Shakespeare performance. For Tunstall, Lecoq's emphasis on '[t]reating the performed playtext like sport, or just fun' can help to free an actor from a strictly language-based approach to characterisation (479). As Edward's Boys actors work feelingly through creating a playworld composed of instinctive, reactive movement, they develop what Tunstall terms a 'proprietorial sense of a shared knowledge of practices and vocabulary' which returns us to Leslie's sense of a shared physical language and, indeed, with Mills's commitment to enabling the boys to 'take over the language' and 'possess it as their own' (Tunstall 480; Mills, 'In the Company' 276). As Tunstall also suggests, such work 'can produce an intensely collaborative social atmosphere' (480): as I watched Edward's Boys working with and off of one another in Leslie's exercise, such an atmosphere was indisputably present.

Such activities would not, however, be possible were it not for the particular collaborative atmosphere the company has long fostered, and Gay McAuley is surely correct in suggesting that exercises such as those described here can also expose us to 'the way the rehearsal experience is embedded within a broader cultural and social context' (214). As I have begun to suggest through my focus on the collective physical understanding created in the Edward's Boys rehearsal room, this broader cultural and social context is a vital component of the company's activities: without it, in fact, the company would almost certainly not have enjoyed the success that it has. Yet what exactly *are* the contexts that give rise to Edward's Boys' productions, and why are they so instrumental to the company's performance of early modern drama?

4 'More of a Sports Team than a Theatre Company': The Ensemble in Performance

When I asked leading Edward's Boys actors to remark upon the dynamic group exercises that made up the movement session I witnessed during preparations for *The Silent Woman*, it was clear that, for them, the notion of 'company' and shared experiences was central to their approach to rehearsal and performance:

NILAY SAH: I think the number one point is it's all about company. Because for a lot of the process, you're in these small collective pockets . . ., and when you see every one of the members of the company all together, and you're doing movement games and things like that, it builds such a strong link, I think.

RITVICK NAGAR: I'd add that Struan specifically focuses on that idea of company, because we don't just do the scenes – the time that we spend on scenes is much smaller than the time we spend working with everyone together, so you do get that physical link with every single person in the company. (personal interview)

Indeed, Leslie himself has confirmed that much of his movement work revolves around developing a tight-knit, cohesive team of performers – for him, 'there's something about that common shared physical vocabulary that goes a long way towards making that ensemble' (personal interview). Recent studies suggest that this kind of shared understanding and strong social bonding between participants is a central tenet in present-day amateur theatre-making. In their *The Ecologies of Amateur Theatre*, Helen Nicholson, Nadine Holdsworth, and Jane Milling argue convincingly for a greater level of recognition of 'the shared knowledge and know-how that amateurs possess' (6). Here, it is worth attending, as these authors do, to 'the friendships and informal networks that [amateur theatre-making] inspires, the ways in which it shapes lives, defines communities and contributes to place-making' – all of these can greatly enhance our understanding of dramatic production in this particular part of the contemporary performance landscape (6). In its less amorphous stock of performers (all boys aged eleven to eighteen) and its more overtly pedagogical outlook, the school-based company is somewhat distinct from the amateur troupes Nicholson and colleagues discuss. Its working practices are nevertheless strikingly similar. As in amateur companies, Edward's Boys' rehearsal and production periods 'carry their own temporal rhythms, and theatre works under the pressure of time; the rhythms of rehearsals define the week, and the annual cycle of auditions and productions often shape the calendar year' (Nicholson, Holdsworth, and Milling 158). For this company, making early modern dramatic performance is 'a social and relational practice reliant on cooperation, collaboration and participation in a shared space', and 'these creative "doings" have the potential to contribute to the construction and sculpting of dynamic communities' (Nicholson, Holdsworth, and Milling 194).

The 'shared space' of KES is a particularly important shaping force on Edward's Boys' practice and fostering of community. Though a state (non-fee-paying) school, KES is a selective grammar: prospective pupils are required to sit a standardised national entry exam (the 'eleven-plus') and to live within a sixteen-mile radius of Stratford-upon-Avon – a radius which encompasses several affluent areas ('Admissions Policy'). This status is important since it determines the profile of not only the average KES pupil but also the average Edward's Boy: the boys who make up the company are drawn from an environment which is itself selective along the lines of educational achievement, aspiration, and, implicitly, class. In their day-to-day school lives, Edward's Boys have access to a wealth of material resources: elite sports activities including rugby, fencing, and rowing, a wide-ranging curriculum which incorporates Classics and specialist languages (to the UK curriculum) such as Mandarin, and regular opportunities to participate in high-profile debating competitions and expensive trips around the world (including, of course, Edward's Boys' international tours).[35] The elite KES environment, that is to say, has important implications for the pool from

---

[35] See 'Academic Curriculum'; 'Extra-Curricular'.

which acting talent is selected, the educational and extra-curricular aspirations of the boys, their sense of their relationship to elite culture, and the space the performance of early modern drama can occupy in their lives.

Put simply, these boys can afford (in all senses of the word) to participate in the elite pastime of early modern dramatic performance. KES's wealth of material resources and emphasis on sport in particular are important contexts for how Edward's Boys approach and describe their participation in the company. The school Sports Department's ethos of '*Participation, Progression, Performance*' is discernible everywhere in the company's activities ('Sport'). Members of the company have long identified 'the camaraderie and support which existed instantaneously' as 'the secret ingredient' to its success (Fielding, qtd. in Mills, 'Re: Interviews'), and Edward's Boys is deliberately populated with boys for whom working as a team comes as second nature. The ensemble necessarily changes year on year as older cast members leave the school (more often than not for university and often, as a further testament of the school's elite status, to Oxford or Cambridge). Renewing the company is therefore a yearly necessity, and, as with the leading professional company Cheek by Jowl, new members of Edward's Boys are not selected by open audition (Kirwan, *Shakespeare in The Theatre* 9). Instead, the ensemble is shaped by the behaviours and aptitudes the boys exhibit in their day-to-day school life. Mills is both the school's deputy head and pastoral lead as well as a teacher of English; he can therefore capitalise on his knowledge of pupils' successes – a compelling speech in assembly, a 'man of the match' award, outstanding reports of class participation – when finding new cast members. This is a nebulous and often vague system of recruitment which, consciously or not, replicates the selective nature of the school itself.

The boys' own comments regarding the ad hoc recruitment process similarly point towards a self-replicating company which fosters a particular 'type'. When asked what they thought it was that made them a suitable candidate for the company's productions, several of the boys identify these characteristics: Waters states that 'You've obviously got to have good teamwork skills, and I think that's the main thing'; Wilkinson remarks that 'a lot of it is to do with leadership – if you're a good leader on the rugby field . . . it'll get translated'; and Hardy identifies the chief question behind an Edward's Boy's recruitment as 'the company – can you fit into that company?' (personal interviews). This notion of 'fitting in', of being identifiable within an already-elite environment as ripe for selection to an elite performance company, is not entirely ahistorical. Recent work on the early modern children's companies, who drew their actors (sometimes by force) from prestigious grammar schools and royal choirs, suggests that those troupes, too, were fashioned in a particular image and capitalised on a privileged skill set (Ackroyd).

In the eyes of the boys as well as their director, these criteria of selection are particularly important for their ability to foster cohesion among the largely homogeneous group. In fact, this element of the company's ethos and performance dynamic supersedes straightforward acting. Joe Pocknell tentatively (and modestly) suggests that while 'we might be alright actors (it's hard to say whether we're good actors or not)', it is 'the company' that is most important.[36] 'At the end of the day', he says, 'it is about us all working together, and the people that bring on the blocks ... are just as important as the people that kill the final person or whatever' (personal interview). Suggesting that the company's approach runs parallel to the operations of a rugby team, in which 'a prop is just as important as a fullback', Pocknell explicitly restates Mills's description of the working conditions he has long striven to foster. Commenting at length on the principles behind his recruitment and rehearsal process, Mills states,

> you don't need the best actors in the world ... But what we
> have is that institution thing behind us. So you don't need
> top actors in every role. You need a spine. It is like a football
> team – you need a really good goalkeeper, one or two top

---

[36] Pocknell appeared in nine productions between 2013 and 2018: as a soldier and ambassador in *Henry V*; Cupid in *Dido, Queen of Carthage*; Cupid in *Galatea*; Spinella in *The Lady's Trial*; Valore in *The Woman Hater*; Bolingbroke in *Will at Westminster*; Pecunius Lucre in *A Trick to Catch the Old One*; Antonio from *Antonio's Revenge* and Malheureux from *The Dutch Courtesan* in the Marston Research in Action event; and Pandora in *The Woman in the Moon*.

central defenders, an amazing midfielder, and a striker. The
rest, you can manage with. (personal interview, 2018)

As far as Pocknell is concerned, Mills's lessons have clearly sunk in. His
easy comparison of the company to an all-male sports team provides further
evidence of the extent to which his participation in the company is inextricably linked to his school life. The forms the boys are asked to fill in
detailing their other commitments for the purposes of rehearsal scheduling,
of which there are dozens in the archive, are cluttered with this kind of
sporting activity. When rehearsing weekly for *The Lady's Trial*, for
instance, Pocknell was alternating the role of Spinella with four fencing
lessons, rugby training, tennis practice, and preparation for the Duke of
Edinburgh award ('Information Sheet'). Given the company's position in
an elite grammar school and its maintenance of a conspicuously all-male
environment, it is unsurprising that in describing this dynamic the boys
return time and again to the analogy of a sports team.

Unlike in much of the professional repertory, Edward's Boys productions are not geared towards shaping a playtext to the talents of star
performers but subjecting a playtext to discernible ensemble practices.
The company's productions capitalise on a veritable hinterland of skills,
implicit training, tacit experience, and learned behaviours – all of which find
a ready home on the stage. It is therefore hardly surprising that the boys
themselves tend to self-identify as sportsmen just as much as actors.
Uncannily echoing Robert Keysar's description of the Children of the
Queen's Revels in 1610 as 'the most expert and skilful actors within the
realm of England . . ., all or most of them trained up in that service in the
reign of the late Queen Elizabeth for ten years *together*' (qtd. in Wickham,
Berry, and Ingram 318, emphasis added), Edward's Boys are a remarkably
tight-knit ensemble. As the comments made by Sah, Nagar, and Leslie
suggest, the physical performance of early modern drama fosters a form of
social cohesion which continuously develops during and between the
rehearsal and performance of individual plays. Like the Children of the
Queen's Revels before them, the company's actors have over the years
grown 'expert and skilful' through their collective performance experience.
Sixty-three per cent of the 159 actors who have worked as part of the

company have taken part multiple times, with an average of between three and four productions per actor. Recent productions in particular have featured a high concentration of remarkably experienced performers: the 2019 production of *The Malcontent* featured a number of actors who have appeared in eight, nine, ten, eleven, or twelve plays, and, later that year, Jack Hawkins, the production's Malevole, set the all-time record by acting in his thirteenth, playing various roles in John Redford's *Wit and Science*. Over the course of their involvement with the company, which often spans the entirety of their school careers, Edward's Boys actors therefore develop a remarkable level of collective performance expertise which easily rivals, if not surpasses, that of British professional companies in which actors come and go with much more regularity.

This emphasis on self-replication and ensemble work does, however, chime with working practices that have been artificially fostered at the RSC. A report produced by the think tank Demos offers detailed insight to the set of ensemble practices, established by Michael Boyd during his tenure as Artistic Director between 2003 and 2012, which helped 'to generate mutual trust and knowledge' between all company personnel 'that would enhance the work on the stage' (Hewison, Holden, and Jones 49). However, as the report suggests, such practices did not develop organically out of pre-existing social structures but through the routine imposition of new artistic and administrative policies and formalised training schemes. In the wake of the company's *Histories* cycle, Boyd suggested that 'our ensemble approach to theatre-making both enables and requires a set of behaviours that are probably worth looking at, because they create our conditions – what we call the conditions for creativity' (qtd. in Radosavljević 149). These operational dynamics and their impact on the performance of Shakespeare have not yet been explored – a book on Boyd's tenure at the RSC is not, for example, currently part of Bloomsbury's Shakespeare in the Theatre series. This feature of Edward's Boys' company identity and shared system of working thus offers a lens through which their performances of early modern drama can be examined – a lens which is not always readily available or analysed on the professional Shakespearean stage.

I suggest that taking such features of Edward's Boys' activities seriously can help us better to understand the performance of early modern drama less as a predominantly text-based exercise and more as a system of behaviours and shared experiences. Indeed, when asked about their work with the company, many members of Edward's Boys suggest that the defining feature of their practice is not the end-product performances but the sense of cohesion and collective endeavour that the *processes* behind such performances necessitate. As in the RSC report, for Edward's Boys, the behaviours and processual knowledge systems to which preparing an early modern play for performance gives rise foster a distinct 'way of being as much as a way of doing' which contributes directly to stage practice (Hewison, Holden, and Jones 18). For Nagar, in fact, 'you become a completely different person doing Edward's Boys' (personal interview). Adopting the terminology of performance theorist Diana Taylor, we might say that what the company characterises as 'our way of working' constitutes a *repertoire* of social and ensemble practices that are brought to bear upon the *archival* early modern playtext. For Taylor, the *repertoire* 'enacts embodied memory: . . . all those acts usually thought of as ephemeral, nonreproducible knowledge . . . The repertoire requires presence: people participate in the production and reproduction of knowledge by "being there", being a part of the transmission' (20). The *archive*, on the other hand, is made up of 'supposedly enduring materials (i.e., texts, documents, buildings, bones)' (18). Taylor identifies a troubling privileging of *archive* over *repertoire*, at least in the Western culture of logocentrism; as I suggested towards the end of Section 1, however, these two modes of performance are for Edward's Boys entirely indivisible. It has long been clear to the company that any performance 'of' the early modern dramatic text is heavily reliant on the learned set of behaviours – or *repertoire* – involved in forming the ensemble, and it is the formation of that ensemble that bleeds discernibly into the fabric of the final text-based performance.

Collaboration, camaraderie, and the ensemble ethos are pervasive throughout Edward's Boys' dramatic activity, particularly the highly physical approach to performance I began to discuss in the previous section. Indeed, the company's strength as an ensemble – discernible even in a moment as microscopic as the comic group rendering of a six-syllable Lylyan line – is frequently remarked upon by academic reviewers, myself included.[37] Observations that the company is 'an ensemble able to interact with energy, intelligence – and impeccable timing' are by no means accidental (Maguire, qtd. in 'Expert Opinion'): indeed, Mills is clear that this approach is vital to a production's success from the very outset of the rehearsal process, setting time aside at 'The Big Meeting' to discuss the company's ethos of 'Trust', 'All together', and 'Apprenticeship' ('*Grobiana's Nuptials* – Big Meeting'). The boys themselves have asserted the importance of this way of working from the outset of the company's formation. Those who took part in the 2008 production of *Dutch Courtesan* note how 'we worked together really well, we were all friends and got on really well, there was a great atmosphere during rehearsals and performances where we all encouraged and supported each other and really gelled together' (Hibberd, qtd. in Mills, 'Re: Interviews').

As is the case with other amateur groups, there are multiple connections between the emotional lives of these schoolboys and their company's working practices and dramatic output.[38] Notably, and perhaps remarkably, the friendships and camaraderie Hibberd describes span the full age range of the company, establishing a profoundly supportive and collaborative approach to rehearsal and performance. Such an approach became evident during a particularly tense get-in for the company's production of *Chaste Maid* in the unfamiliar space of Somerville College chapel in Oxford. Having left the boys to reblock the play on their own once he had realised that 'this isn't working', Mills observed from a concealed part of the college chapel that 'what was happening was what I'd hoped would happen, which is the older kids ... pulled them together' (personal interview, 2018). As Harry Davies, the production's Allwit, recalls,

> in the two hours before we went on, we pulled ourselves together. In the tightly packed room of shivering bodies we went through, in whispers, virtually in silence, which entrance our props had to come on from:

[37] See Jowett; McCarthy, 'Review of *The Woman Hater*' 721 and 'Review of *Summer's Last Will*' 329; Smith, 'Review: *Henry V*'.

[38] See Nicholson, Holdsworth, and Milling 180–3.

'Promoter's basket – [entrance] one or [entrance] two?'
'One.'
'Crucifix – one or two?'
'Two.'

And it went on like this with a hypnotic effect. It was either 'One' or 'Two' because that was all we had. We did it though, we got the job done – a relatively simple task but it brought us together and made us focus on what needed to be achieved. ('Look Back in Gender')

'Pulling together', that is, sowed the seeds for a mutual understanding of the physical shape of the performance, right down to the direction of travel of the production's mass of props. Since then, an established pattern of knowledge transfer has become common currency for company members of all ages. Recalling his progression through company ranks, Dan Wilkinson relates that taking on minor (sometimes silent roles) upon entry to the troupe is

the whole point – you're just there to learn on the job, effectively. I remember, looking back, there was Jeremy Franklin, Alex Mills, Harry Davies, and these guys were incredible human beings. There was a real role model kind of thing going on, at least that's what I found ... I learnt a lot from just watching them act and seeing how they went through the process. I learnt how to act from those guys. (personal interview)

Likewise, upon leaving the company, Wilkinson's fellow 'ten-play lads' remarked that

the most important thing of all is that these lessons were taught to me and my fellow '09-ers, not by 'Sir' or 'Miss', but by our mates. By being in the company, we had been in the presence of boys far older, more mature and better than ourselves right from the start of our school lives. We could not have helped but learn something from them. (Hatch et al., 'Exit')

Wilkinson and his colleagues describe a remarkably organic performance environment in which the transfer of knowledge from performer to performer, body to body, underpins the more overt enterprise of bringing the early modern playtext 'to life'. Such an environment aligns closely with what Pierre Nora terms '*milieux de mémoire*' ('environments of memory') in which culture is retained and transferred in oral and corporeal forms (13; see also Roach 26). Evident throughout the boys' description of this dynamic is how difficult its specific nature is to pin down and all the more so to create artificially. As a more recent Edward's Boys graduate, Charlie Waters, explains, once an actor begins to take on the 'apprentice master' role later in his career, 'you don't necessarily teach the younger kids what to do . . . It sounds kind of top-down teaching, but it's not so much that. I never say we actively tell people what to do . . . it's hard to explain' (personal interview). Indeed, the lack of a systematic approach to apprenticeship within the company is so self-regulated as to evade easy description and categorisation. Over the course of my interviews with Mills and the boys, I discovered that Mills is sometimes unaware of specific working patterns. Jamie Mitchell, one of the youngest company members when I interviewed him in 2018, confidently described himself as 'an apprentice' to Jack Hawkins, who 'teaches me everything' (personal interview).[39] When I relayed this to

---

[39] Hawkins appeared in thirteen productions between 2013 and 2019: as a member of the chorus in *Dido, Queen of Carthage*; Robin in *Galatea*; Levidolce in *The Lady's Trial*; Oriana in *The Woman Hater*; Henry V in *Unperfect Actors*; Richard II in *Will at Westminster*; Witgood in *A Trick to Catch the Old One*; Autumn in *Summer's Last Will and Testament*; Prologue from *Antonio and Mellida*, Feliche from *Antonio's Revenge*, and Franceschina from *The Dutch Courtesan* in the Marston Research in Action event; Prologus and Gunophilus in *The Woman in the Moon*; Prologus from *The Woman in the Moon* and Antonio from *Antonio's Revenge* in *When Paul's Boys Met Edward's Boys*; Malevole in *The Malcontent*; and various roles in *Wit and Science*. His 'apprentice', Mitchell, has acted in eight productions to date: as Silence from *Henry IV* in Unperfect Actors; Gentleman, Boy, and Huntsman in *A Trick to Catch the Old One*; Epilogue in *Summer's Last Will and Testament*; Balurdo from *Antonio and Mellida* and Boy from *Antonio's Revenge* in the Marston Research in Action event; Luna in *The Woman in the Moon*; Luna from *The Woman in the Moon* and Mistress Honeysuckle from

Mills, expecting him to clarify that he had arranged the partnership, he replied that it was 'news to me. But isn't that great?' (personal interview, 2018). As Hawkins, then in his final year at school, later explained, the relationship between the two boys reaches far beyond a unidirectional model of instruction and imitation:

> Well, we joke about the apprenticeship thing a lot, and I say, 'you can be my apprentice', and stuff like that. I talk to him – he's a really nice kid, he's brilliant, we get on quite well, and he's a really good actor, a good speaker … It's not really as though I'm imparting my wisdom or anything like that – I don't even talk to him about acting, to be honest. We get on, we do stuff … He could talk to me. They all could. But I specifically get on with Jamie quite well. (personal interview)

For the company, however, this form of shared learning is not unidirectional. As Wilkinson puts it, 'We used to discuss … whether it's like a conveyor belt, but it's not so much that … The younger boys learn from the older boys, the older boys learn from the younger boys, too … that's the way that it works' (personal interview). Rory Gopsill also describes the need to 'get over the age differential … you move past it because you're there to get the job done' (personal interview).[40] This job, Adam Hardy explains, 'requires a really delicate balance of support and teamwork between each person, and that is a kind of horizontal and vertical level of integration – between the different years as well, so, supporting people around you who are playing similar parts' (personal interview).[41] Pascal Vogiaridis suggests that this

---

Westward Ho! in *When Paul's Boys Met Edward's Boys*; Emilia in *The Malcontent*; and Sir John Daw in *The Silent Woman*.

[40] Gopsill appeared in four productions between 2016 and 2018: as Tantoblin in *Grobiana's Nuptials*; Walkadine Hoard in *A Trick to Catch the Old One*; Summer in *Summer's Last Will and Testament*; and Antonio from *Antonio and Mellida* and Freevill from *The Dutch Courtesan* in the Marston Research in Action event.

[41] Hardy took part in eight productions between 2013 and 2018: as the French Ambassador in *Henry V*; Ericthinis in *Galatea*; Prologue and Epilogue in *The*

multidirectional form of integration may be influenced by Mills's introduction of the 'vertical tutoring system' at the school, in which boys from
all year groups share communal spaces and pastoral classes (personal
interview) – yet another example of performance practice being under-
girded by wider social systems and daily rhythms.[42] Throughout my
observations of Edward's Boys in rehearsal, I have routinely witnessed
these affective bonds between boys of all ages being realised in the act of
putting on a play.

During the get-in at St Paul's Cathedral, for instance, in the breaks
between scene runs I watched Vogiaridis taking younger members to one
side once they had exited to model how to leap onto the stage (including
Dutton's 'hitting it big and loud' when entering his scene in *Chaste Maid*) or
seductively pick a handkerchief up off the floor.[43] When, during a run-
through of the killing of Julio in act three, scene one of *Antonio's Revenge*,
the 'blood condom' the young Tom Howitt had concealed beneath his
costume refused to burst at the right time, company members of all ages
rallied around him to assess the best way to carry out the move. In these
moments, the boys' collaborative team practices were brought to the fore,
right from the collective 'mucking in' involved in the whole cast carrying
props and instruments across the Thames to the physical warm-ups – led by
older members of the cast – and self-directed run-throughs of entrances and
exits to the pre-show 'huddle' minutes before the boys took to the stage.

Lady's Trial; Gentleman and Servant in *The Woman Hater*; Hunch in *Grobiana's
Nuptials*; Onesiphorus Hoard in *A Trick to Catch the Old One*; Jupiter in *The
Woman in the Moon*; and Jupiter from *The Woman in the Moon*, Ericthinis from
Galatea, and Summer from *Summer's Last Will and Testament* in *When Paul's
Boys Met Edward's Boys*.

[42] Vogiaridis acted in nine productions between 2013 and 2018: as John Bates in
Henry V; Hermes in *Dido, Queen of Carthage*; Phillida in *Galatea*; Adurni in *The
Lady's Trial*; Mercer in *The Woman Hater*; Host in *A Trick to Catch the Old One*;
Vertumnus in *Summer's Last Will and Testament*; Melos in *The Woman in the
Moon*; and Lord Kix from *A Chaste Maid in Cheapside* in *When Paul's Boys Met
Edward's Boys*.

[43] Vogiaridis was at this point one of the company's most senior members and
KES's Head Boy.

Recounting these rehearsals in particular, Hardy and Vogiaridis were quick to point out the sporting ethos that underpinned these activities. For the company, sport and theatre are directly interrelated in fostering the close-ness and collaborative dynamic that its members pinpoint as essential to the dramatic enterprise – a dynamic which, as old boy Tom Sharp puts it on the company's website, may well have been 'shared by the original boys' companies' ('The Spirit').

These close interpersonal dynamics and the learning of performance craft they facilitate constitute a form of what Paul Connerton refers to as '*incorporating* practice', in which knowledge becomes 'sedimented in the body' (72). Such practice chimes readily with the 'cognitive ecology' model of early modern performance proposed by Evelyn Tribble. In her discus-sion of early modern acting companies, Tribble convincingly argues for 'the crucial role of the social embodiment and embeddedness of agents within a complex system' (113) – too often a site of neglect in theatre history. For Tribble, the social development of corporeal expertise 'ultimately give[s] shape and form to the plays' (111). In their reliance on tacit instruction, embodied knowledge systems, and a collaborative approach to perfor-mance, then, Edward's Boys may constitute a surprisingly close analogue to early modern performance practice. The bold experimentation and physicalisation to which this approach opens up the playtexts therefore merits the close attention of anyone studying these underperformed dramatic works.

On the stage, the close social dynamics of Edward's Boys pay dividends in the company's ability to co-ordinate with one another on the fly. During a performance of *The Malcontent* at Trinity College, Oxford in 2019, Nagar's Mendoza attempted to throw a ring up to Hawkins's Malevole, looming on the balcony, and missed altogether, prompting a comically exasperated – and unscripted – eye-roll from Hawkins.[44] When he re-entered the scene

---

[44] Mendoza's line in the printed text – 'Here, take my ring unto the citadel' (4.3.91) – does not explicitly demand that the ring be thrown – nor, in fact, does the scene suggest that Malevole is positioned on a higher level. Edward's Boys' realisation of the moment thus constitutes a typical physical interpolation to the playtext that entertained even when it backfired.

moments later, Hawkins adjusted Malevole's opening line – 'Your devilship's ring has no virtue' (4.3.118) – to, 'Seeing as your devilship throwest like a girl, your ring has no virtue.' Nagar, po-faced, retorted, 'It is 2019. We do not compare boys' throws to those of girls.' As Mills revealed in a subsequent question and answer session, the entire moment was unscripted, the inventive adjustment of the playtext entirely down to Hawkins and Nagar – two actors who have frequently joked about jostling for pre-eminence in the company in rehearsals and interviews. The company's dynamic, and the two actors' profound friendship in particular, facilitates silent communication, intimate shared knowledge, and quicksilver adjustments to physical and vocal delivery – none of which are recoverable from an inspection of the printed playtext but all of which are essential to its successful reiteration in performance.

For the company, the ethos of camaraderie and teamwork has a tangible influence over the performance of an early modern play, particularly as it relates to the analogy of sport which Mills 'always uses' (Hatch, *Film Extracts*). According to Wilkinson, the practices of sport and theatre are inseparable. Reading both rugby and theatre as 'an execution of a trained task', he suggests that keeping a foot in both camps helps to develop 'chemistry on stage and off stage. Very few people, as a company, have that rapport. There are just things that you know . . . if you'd played with Fin on a rugby field as scrum half for seven years, you know that he's going to pitch left – you can just tell' (personal interview). Wilkinson identifies a profound level of shared corporeal knowledge among company members, and this awareness of one another's individual movements and thought processes seems to allow for intensely collaborative performances which extend beyond anything explicitly prompted or pre-empted by the written text.

Since, as Hawkins noted to me, Edward's Boys often feels 'more like a sports team than a theatre company' (personal interview), it makes sense that overlapping practices can be identified in their preparation and performance of an early modern play. If, for Wilkinson, dramatic performance is the same as 'when you're on a rugby field, executing the moves you've trained in a million times before', we might envisage the Edward's Boys stage as itself a sporting arena. Sport is sometimes conceived of as a central feature of a production from Mills's initial brainstorming sessions – his preliminary notes for *The Woman Hater* in 2016, for instance, include the suggestions 'Like fencing, sport' and '<u>All of us together</u>' ('WH Notes') – and the ethos frequently carries right through to the final production stages. *The Woman Hater*, for example, was indeed characterised by endless motion, with characters from principals to supernumeraries scuttling across the stage to develop a sense of what Mills referred to in rehearsal schedules as 'the busy-ness of Milan' ('Sunday 14th February').

As early as *The Dutch Courtesan* in 2008, these dynamics were being put to productive use. Throughout the performance, boys leapt energetically into one other's arms, picked one another up into fireman's lifts, and threw small props to one another from the upstage balcony (all of which, unlike Nagar's ring, were virtuosically caught). In the post-performance discussion, Carol Chillington Rutter was quick to point out this physical aspect of the production, noting with astonishment how the boys 'caught *everything*' that was thrown to them and ascribing this talent to her own observations of the boys' endless games of throwing and catching in the school playground. Since then, there have been regular instances when the sport and physical display that comes naturally to the actors fuses seamlessly with dramatic performance. The rugby-based style of movement which underpinned *Henry V* in 2013, for instance, was, according to Henry Edwards, a direct result of the captain of the school's first XV, Nick Edmonds, being among the cast (personal interview). This involvement resulted in striking stage images: in addition to the rugby lineout lifting Henry into the air I mentioned in the Introduction, the boys came together in a scrum formation to signify the army marching through the battlefield and represented hand-to-hand combat through rucks on the stage floor. These motifs constituted a particularly forceful blending of *archive* and *repertoire* – the Shakespearean text being overlaid, underscored, and indeed remade by extratextual corporeal practices and ways of being.

Through this approach, each Edward's Boys production becomes a great deal more than a performance 'of' an early modern play: the company's stage activity is just as much about performing *as* 'Edward's Boys'. Indeed, those members of the company with very few lines – typically the newest and youngest recruits – will often come to know 'the company' before they know 'the play', the kind of ensemble movement work I have been describing providing their main point of access to the production. The application of physical practices from elsewhere in the boys' lives – particularly the rugby pitch and the gymnasium – is central to the collaborative processes by which Leslie and the boys undertake the enterprise of what he calls 'physicalising the milieu of the production' (personal interview). For Leslie, creating the 'physical world' of an early modern play 'is about using what you've got in front of you' – just as it may have been for the boy companies of centuries gone by (personal interview). This infiltration of playtext with pre-existing corporeal knowledge and group expertise becomes all the more prominent when dealing, as the company typically does, with the non-Shakespearean (anti-)canon. These non-canonical texts, with a less stable (often non-existent) *archive* of past performances, critical interventions, and even editions, arguably stand to benefit yet more greatly from the somewhat ungraspable *repertoire* of embodied practices and knowledge systems that have become such a central part of Edward's Boys' practice.

The effects of such practice are particularly prominent in what has become a key feature of the company's 'house style': the use of a non-verbal, often highly virtuosic, movement sequence at the very outset of the performance which sets the physical tone of the production. A finalised form of the physical experimentation undertaken in rehearsal, these sequences – which, borrowing from contemporary television, we might term 'cold opens'[45] – bring extratextual physicality and company spirit into highly productive collision with the world of the playtext. At the outset of the 2009 *A Mad World, My Masters*, for instance, electric guitar music blared over the speakers as seven boys marched onto the stage, each holding a wooden chair or stool of various designs, and began to 'build the set' by setting them down. Four punks – the play's team of tricksters – entered and swaggered with abandon about the space, knocking the chairs over and leaping on top of them as more chairs were brought onto the stage. When the music stopped abruptly, they slouched down into the last chairs standing and launched into the play's first scene. The 2010 production of *A Chaste Maid in Cheapside* began in similar – though less reckless – fashion, with the entire company standing in formation to sing a hymn before dispersing and milling about the stage space and through the three-sided auditorium, the

---

[45] See Pollick.

hymn giving way to the cries of Cheapside's costermongers. Older members of the cast brought in the individual staging units which would form the production's set, being stacked into towers or arranged into separate beds, coffins, or podia as befitted individual scenes. Even in these early productions, a sense of the playtext's subjugation to youthful physicality and ensemble movement was beginning to be felt.

As the company have strengthened and developed their distinctive way of working, these sequences have become more ambitious, as in the opening of the 2017 production of *A Trick to Catch the Old One*. In the text, the penniless Witgood's accrual of debts is announced by the opening line 'All's gone!' (1.1.1). Here, it was conveyed through a bravura set piece known as the 'fleecing sequence'. As the lights came up, Hawkins's Witgood, dressed in tight jeans and a fringed leather jacket, swaggered onto the black box stage, everything from his startling Mohican to his scuffed leather boots emanating the 1970s cool of the simple set that surrounded him – a real-life Sex Pistols album cover brought to life through blown-up images of playing cards, poker chips, and cigarettes. Stopping centre stage, and without breaking the spectators' gaze, he raised a tassel-sleeved arm and snapped his fingers, bringing the onstage band's drummer to life as the stage erupted into a punk-rock number. A series of younger boys scurried onto the stage, handing Witgood slips of paper and 'wine' to be knocked back from a plastic cup. More boys swarmed the space, ranging from six-foot-stupid and bulky to remarkably diminutive, dressed as young women, old men, and everything in between. Witgood grabbed one of the 'pretty girls' (the production's Joyce, played by Felix Kerrison-Adams) by the waist and swung her around him, while the rest of the cast danced with reckless abandon. As the music swelled, the ensemble turned on Witgood, grasping at him and removing his necklaces and rings. Riches looted, they retreated in groups to the four corners of the stage, each team effortlessly raising its smallest member into the air. They flocked back centre stage and systematically – though chaotically – undressed Witgood: small boys pulling off his boots and tossing them away, others gleefully tugging off his jacket and pulling down his jeans. Modesty preserved by only a scant pair of shorts and ankle socks, Witgood was raised into the air with a cheer, and the swarm departed, leaving him alone, trembling, locking his knees together, covering his crotch with his hands, and squeaking the opening line of Middleton's play (see Figure 6).

The seamless fusing of sport and physical display with the early modern playtext is such a defining feature of the company's practice that it occasionally provides the backdrop for the entire production. In the 2013 *Dido, Queen of Carthage*, pervasive physicality was taken to the extreme from the outset: at the play's opening, a gym teacher's whistle was blown, upon which a chorus of young boys in white vests and shorts jogged through the audience, stopping to leapfrog over one another in quick succession. Throughout the performance, this chorus would continue physically to realise the fictional world of Marlowe and Nashe's play at the sound of the whistle, with one of the boys, for instance, cartwheeling into a handstand, held up by his fellows, in order to create the 'bush' in which Venus hides (1.1.139). As Brett D. Hirsch noted in his review of the production, such moments saw '[e]ven cast members playing minor roles work[ing] together admirably – literally coming together when forming human pyramids alongside other displays of acrobatic teamwork to

Figure 6 Jack Hawkins as Witgood and the Edward's Boys ensemble in the 2017 production of Thomas Middleton's *A Trick to Catch the Old One*, directed by Perry Mills. Photo by Lauren Hyslop, courtesy of Edward's Boys.

represent physical structures' ('Review: *Dido*'). Both Dido's cave and the fire into which she casts herself at the play's climax were constructed via smaller boys clambering nimbly onto the shoulders of their larger fellows with a swiftness and ease that bespoke the collaborative atmosphere which pervades the rehearsal process. Such a dynamic was clearly envisaged from the earliest stages of rehearsal: the company's archive contains a series of sketches, appended to photographs of mid-century acrobatic and sports teams, which correspond directly to several of the tableaux mounted by the boys in performance (see Figures 7 and 8). The same strategy would be adopted in the company's 2014 production of *Galatea*, when, for example, Hebe's tree was represented by boys sitting atop or standing on their older acting fellows (see Figure 9).[46]

We can, of course, be fairly certain that the original performances of these plays did not see the Children of Paul's or the Queen's Revels clambering onto one another's shoulders every time scenery was called for – though it might be instructive to remember that Jonson's *Poetaster* demands, in one scene, that in the dramatic display put on by Captain Tucca's two *pyrgi* one of them stands on the other's shoulders (3.4.279 SD).[47] What I do wish to emphasise, however, is that, in the Edward's Boys rehearsal rooms and performances I have discussed here, the sporting ethos of the school's environment repeatedly reshapes he playtext, remaking and indeed supplanting the author's words through ensemble practice and onstage physicality. The company dynamics and physical skill sets I have discussed here allow Edward's Boys to revel in the non-textual even when approaching the most wordy of early modern plays. Despite their tireless tablework and emphasis on textual fidelity, it is arguably this dimension of their performances that is the most compelling – an 'infection' of text with stage embodiment and teamwork which allows contemporary audiences to

---

[46] For a review of the production, see Kesson, 'Review: *Galatea*'. For my discussion of similar moments of stagecraft, much of them repeated from these earlier productions, in the more recent *When Paul's Boys Met Edward's Boys*, see McCarthy, 'Review: *When Paul's Boys*'.

[47] Though the explicit stage direction only appears in the 1616 folio rendering of the text, the quarto of 1602 provides just as much scope for this particular bit of stagecraft.

Figure 7 One of Perry Mills's initial tableau sketches for the company's 2013 production of Christopher Marlowe and Thomas Nashe's *Dido, Queen of Carthage*, held in the company's archive. Photo by Harry R. McCarthy, reproduced with permission.

grasp the theatrical nature of these plays. Creating a performance dynamic in which the virtuosic bodies of actors are insistently foregrounded through ensemble practice and the effortless incorporation of physical skill, time and again Team Edward's Boys kick the authors of these plays back onto the

Figure 8 Dan Wilkinson as Dido with the ensemble realising the above sketch in the 2013 production of Christopher Marlowe and Thomas Nashe's *Dido, Queen of Carthage*, directed by Perry Mills. Photo by David Troughton, courtesy of Edward's Boys.

Figure 9 Members of the Edward's Boys ensemble forming Hebe's tree in the 2014 production of John Lyly's *Galatea*, directed by Perry Mills. Photo by Mark Ellis, courtesy of Edward's Boys.

bench – whether he be Christopher Marlowe, John Redford, or, indeed, William Shakespeare.

Conclusion

In her 'Company Profile' on the Edward's Boys website, Laurie Maguire begins by pitting the work of the company against the predominant tradition of Shakespeare performance, invoking a well-worn theatre-historical comparison in order to do so: 'When the travelling players show up in Hamlet's Elsinore, they complain about a rival theatre attraction that is drawing big audiences: the newly fashionable boys' companies. With Edward's Boys, modern audiences and scholars can understand – for the first time in 400 years – the draw of these "little eyases"' ('Company Profile'). The work of Edward's Boys, she suggests, can help audiences and theatre historians today to grasp 'why the adult players in *Hamlet* were forced out of town'. For Maguire, the unique means of access they provide to a wide range of theatrically vibrant early modern drama offers a sustained challenge to the contemporary, adult, Shakespearean stage. In this Element, it has not been my aim to suggest that Edward's Boys present a threat to the present-day landscape of Shakespeare performance, however favourably academic reviewers tend to compare their productions to those at 'the rather larger theatres around the corner' (see Pérez Díez, 'Review of *The Malcontent*'). Rather, I have suggested that the work of Edward's Boys has *shifted* that landscape, providing us with a more open, playful means of access to a number of critically understudied (and under-performed) non-Shakespearean plays. Edward's Boys' current lifespan is roughly as long as that of any early modern boys' company. In that time, they have created a new early modern performance canon which allows us not only to experience some of the theatrical thrill of watching these plays performed by young actors but also to access the kinds of behaviour, physical skills, and ensemble expertise to which those plays give rise.

Maguire's comparison of Edward's Boys with the real-life early modern 'little eyases' implicitly raises the inevitable question: to what extent can the work of the company allow us to access the theatrical past? I have aimed to steer clear of the kind of 'would have' scholarship that draws a direct equivalence between present-day practice and historical performance.

Perry Mills is not Richard Mulcaster; Jack Hawkins bears little resemblance to Nathan Field. Yet the rehearsal and performance practices of Edward's Boys do, in some way, engage with the past through the negotiations they continuously initiate between text and body, the company's actors confronting – sometimes for the first time in four centuries – the opportunities the material traces of theatre history present to the making of performance. Watching as centuries-old plays are worked with, and worked upon, through close physical collaboration can, I submit, allow us fleetingly to grasp at the material exigencies of past performance processes. In Edward's Boys, the close-knit troupe of performing bodies becomes a powerful technology of historical enquiry, engaging and reshaping the texts of a long-gone theatrical era for audiences today.

That close-knit troupe is paramount to Edward's Boys' theatrical activity, giving rise to the kind of shared processual knowledge and collective approach to performance that theatre history is beginning to understand as characteristic of early modern acting companies. Throughout this Element, I have insistently prioritised 'company' over 'playtext' – a practice which is entirely consistent with the approach Edward's Boys take to rehearsal and performance. Engaging closely with the specific social system that undergirds the company's performances has at least as much to tell us about performing early modern drama today as any inspection of the playtext, or indeed any observation of a final public performance. Through their engagement with early modern drama, Edward's Boys have developed distinct systems of behaviour, communal knowledge, and group expertise: it is no exaggeration to say that, for them, performing the plays of Shakespeare's contemporaries, and indeed Shakespeare, is nothing short of a way of being. As this way of being has developed, the performance of an early modern play (even *Henry V*) has become a means of performing the company in an overt display of physical virtuosity, camaraderie, and collective identity that allows us to shift our perspective of what these plays actually 'are' in performance. For Edward's Boys, an early modern play is, and a always has been, a site of body work, a place for physical experimentation, and a means of developing company identity through ensemble play and shared endeavour. To the boys, it is perfectly obvious that early modern drama should be approached in this way. Perhaps it is time that we approached it in that way, too.

Appendix

Edward's Boys Productions, 2005–20

Production Year	Play/Performance	Performance Venues	Early Performance History[1]	Recent UK Revivals[2]
2005	*Elizabethan Boy Players: The Thisby Project* (extracts by William Shakespeare and Ben Jonson)	King Edward VI School	—	—
2008	*The Dutch Courtesan*, by John Marston (Acts 1–3)	University of Warwick; King Edward VI School; Dulwich College; Shakespeare's Globe	1604: Children of the Queen's Revels at the Blackfriars 1606: Children of the Queen's Revels at Greenwich Palace 1613: Lady Elizabeth's Men at Whitehall Palace 1620: Prince Charles's Men at the Cockpit (?)	1964: National Theatre (dir. William Gaskill and Piers Haggard)
2009	*Endymion*, by John Lyly (extracts)	King Edward VI School; Shakespeare's Globe	1588: Children of Paul's at Paul's Playhouse and Greenwich Palace	2002: Globe Education at Bear Gardens Theatre ('Read Not Dead' reading, dir. James Wallace)

[1] I base these early stage histories on those provided by Wiggins and Richardson.

[2] Details of professional performances to 2010 are taken from Karin Brown's Appendix in Aebischer and Prince. I additionally provide the number of recorded amateur productions, based on Jeremy Lopez's Appendix in the same volume. I have supplemented this information with more recent productions recorded in the online archives of UK theatres, and through private consultation with Shakespeare's Globe's Read Not Dead director, James Wallace.

2009	*A Mad World, My Masters*, by Thomas Middleton	University of Warwick; Balliol College, Oxford; King Edward VI School	1605: Children of Paul's at Paul's Playhouse 1632–40: Queen Henrietta's or Prince Charles's Men at Salisbury Court	1998: Shakespeare's Globe (dir. Sue Lefton) 2013: Royal Shakespeare Company at the Swan (dir. Sean Foley)
2010	*A Chaste Maid in Cheapside*, by Thomas Middleton	King's College, London; Somerville College, Oxford; King Edward VI School	1613: Lady Elizabeth's Men at the Swan	1997: Shakespeare's Globe (dir. Malcolm McKay) 2002: Almeida and UK tour (dir. Ben Harrison) 20 amateur revivals between 1912 and 2013
2010	*Mother Bombie*, by John Lyly (extracts)	Magdalen College, Oxford; King Edward VI School; Shakespeare's Globe	1589: Children of Paul's at Paul's Playhouse	2010: Globe Education at Bear Gardens Theatre ('Read Not Dead' reading, dir. James Wallace)

Cont.

Production Year	Play/Performance	Performance Venues	Early Performance History[1]	Recent UK Revivals[2]
2011	*Antonio's Revenge*, by John Marston	Wadham College, Oxford; King Edward VI School; Middle Temple Hall	1600: Children of Paul's at Paul's Playhouse	1979: adapted as *Antonio* at Nottingham Playhouse (dir. Peter Barnes and Geoffrey Reeves) 2000: Globe Education at Bear Gardens Theatre ('Read Not Dead' reading, dir. James Wallace) 1 amateur revival in 1984
2012	*Westward Ho!*, by Thomas Dekker and John Webster	King Edward VI School; Lady Margaret Hall, Oxford; Faculty of English, University of Cambridge; King's College, London	1604: Children of Paul's at Paul's Playhouse	1995: Globe Education at Bear Gardens Theatre ('Read Not Dead' reading, dir. Samuel West) 2008: Paper and String at White Bear Theatre (dir. Andrea Kantor)
2013	*Henry V*, by William Shakespeare	King Edward VI School; RSC Swan Theatre	1599: Lord Chamberlain's Men at the Curtain 1605: King's Men at Whitehall Palace	Countless: see Smith, *King Henry V*

| 2013 | *Dido, Queen of Carthage*, by Christopher Marlowe and Thomas Nashe | King Edward VI School; Christ Church College, Oxford | 1588: Children of the Chapel Royal (on tour?) | 1964: Nuffield Theatre (dir. Jocelyn Powell)
2003: Shakespeare's Globe (dir. Tim Carroll)
2006–8: angels in the architecture at The House and Chapel of St Barnabas-in-Soho (2006) and the State Apartments, Kensington Palace (2007–8)
2009: National Theatre (dir. James Macdonald)
2015: Globe Young Players at the Sam Wanamaker Playhouse (dir. Jacqui Somerville)
2017: Royal Shakespeare Company at the Swan (dir. Kimberley Sykes) |

Cont.

Production Year	Play/Performance	Performance Venues	Early Performance History[1]	Recent UK Revivals[2]
2014	*Galatea*, by John Lyly	Lady Margaret Hall, Oxford; Queen Mary's Grammar School; King Edward VI School; Playbox Theatre; Sam Wanamaker Playhouse	1588: Children of Paul's at Greenwich Palace	2007: Globe Education at Bear Gardens Theatre ('Read Not Dead' reading, dir. James Wallace)
2015	*The Lady's Trial*, by John Ford	Lady Margaret Hall, Oxford; Queen Mary's Grammar School; King Edward VI School; Sam Wanamaker Playhouse	1638: Beeston's Boys at the Cockpit	—
2016	*The Woman Hater*, by Francis Beaumont	The Other Place, RSC; University of Oxford Catholic Chaplaincy; King's College, London; Collège L'Assomption, Montpellier; Maison des Chœurs, Montpellier; SortieOuest, Béziers	1606: Children of Paul's at Paul's Playhouse 1630: Children of the King's Revels at Salisbury Court (?) 1630s: King's Men at the Globe and/or Blackfriars	1 amateur revival in 2002
2016	*Unperfect Actors* (extracts by William Shakespeare)	King Edward VI School	—	—

2016	*Will at Westminster* (extracts from *Richard II*, by William Shakespeare)	Westminster Hall	—	—
2016	*Grobiana's Nuptials*, by Charles May	King Edward VI School; Magdalen College, Oxford	1637: Students of St John's College, Oxford	—
2017	*A Trick to Catch the Old One*, by Thomas Middleton	Lady Margaret Hall, Oxford; King Edward VI School; University College London	1605: Children of Paul's at Paul's Playhouse 1606–8: Children of the Queen's Revels at the Blackfriars 1607: Children of the Queen's Revels at Whitehall Palace	1978: Theatre Clywd 1985: Wayward Players at Bear Gardens Theatre (dir. Diane West) 2007: Globe Education at Bear Gardens Theatre ('Read Not Dead' reading, dir. James Wallace)
2017	*Summer's Last Will and Testament*, by Thomas Nashe	King Edward VI School; Sam Wanamaker Playhouse; The Old Palace School	1592: Children of the Chapel or Paul's (?) at Croydon Palace	—
2017	*Research in Action: The Marston Project* (extracts by John Marston)	King Edward VI School; Sam Wanamaker Playhouse	—	—

Cont.

Production Year	Play/Performance	Performance Venues	Early Performance History[1]	Recent UK Revivals[2]
2018	*The Woman in the Moon*, by John Lyly	Lady Margaret Hall, Oxford; St-Mary-at-Hill, Eastcheap; King Edward VI School; The Dream Factory; Théâtre d'O, Montpellier; Maison des Chœurs, Montpellier; SortieOuest, Béziers	1588: Children of Paul's at Paul's Playhouse 1589/90: Children of Paul's at Richmond Palace (?)	2007: Globe Education at Bear Gardens Theatre ('Read Not Dead' reading, dir. James Wallace) 2014: The Dolphin's Back at the Rose Playhouse (dir. James Wallace) 2017: The Dolphin's Back at the Sam Wanamaker Playhouse (dir. James Wallace)
2018	*When Paul's Boys Met Edward's Boys* (extracts by Dekker and Webster, Jonson, Lyly, Marlowe, Marston, Middleton, and Nashe, in collaboration with the choir of St Paul's Cathedral)	St Paul's Cathedral; Sam Wanamaker Playhouse	—	—

| 2019 | *The Malcontent*, by John Marston | King Edward VI School, Stratford-upon-Avon; St-Mary-at-Hill, Eastcheap; Trinity College, Oxford | 1603: Children of the Queen's Revels at the Blackfriars 1604: King's Men at the Globe 1635: King's Men at the Blackfriars | 1996: Globe Education at Bear Gardens Theatre ('Read Not Dead' reading, dir. Timothy West) 2002: Royal Shakespeare Company at the Swan/Newcastle Playhouse/Gielgud Theatre (dir. Dominic Cooke) 2014: Globe Young Players at the Sam Wanamaker Playhouse (dir. Caitlin McLeod) |
| 2019 | *Wit and Science*, by John Redford | King Edward VI School; New College, Oxford; The Priory Church of the Order of St John, Clerkenwell; Palazzo Ducale, Genoa | 1534–47: Children of Paul's (?)[3] – | |

3 See Twycross.

Cont.

Production Year	Play/Performance	Performance Venues	Early Performance History[1]	Recent UK Revivals[2]
2020	*The Silent Woman, or Epicene,* by Ben Jonson	Cancelled due to Covid-19. Released as a podcast in 2020 (see McCarthy, 'The One that Got Away')	1610: Children of the Queen's Revels at the Whitefriars 1620: Prince Charles's Men at the Cockpit (?) 1636: King's Men at the Blackfriars 1636: King's Men at St James's Palace and the Cockpit in Court	1989: Royal Shakespeare Company at the Swan (dir. Danny Boyle) 15 amateur revivals between 1885 and 2013

References

Archival Materials

Note: The Edward's Boys Archive, held in the Memorial Library at King Edward VI School in Stratford-upon-Avon, is a rather informally organised affair, and its contents, which occupy around forty box files and ring binders, are not arranged by shelf mark or catalogue number. I have tried to be as specific as possible in my description of each item in the hope that subsequent researchers can access the materials with relative ease.

Bowen, Harry, Jeremy Franklin, George Matts, and Perry Mills. 'Script for Talk at Summerfields School, Oxford'. 2011. Edward's Boys Archive, King Edward VI School, Stratford-upon-Avon, *Elizabethan Boy Players* Box 1.

Doran, Gregory. 'Comments'. 2017. Edward's Boys Archive, King Edward VI School, Stratford-upon-Avon, *A Trick to Catch the Old One* Box 2.

Edwards, Henry. Annotated script for *Antonio's Revenge*. 2011. Edwards Family Private Collection, Stratford-upon-Avon.

Annotated script for *Henry V*. 2013. Edwards Family Private Collection, Stratford-upon-Avon.

'Emails'. 2019. Edward's Boys Archive, King Edward VI School, Stratford-upon-Avon, *The Malcontent* Box 1.

Hayes, Oliver. 'CAPITAL Centre – Evaluation'. 2010. Edward's Boys Archive, King Edward VI School, Stratford-upon-Avon, *A Chaste Maid in Cheapside* Folder 1.

Leslie, Struan. 'Moving Lyly'. *Galatea*. Programme. Edward's Boys, 2014. Edward's Boys Archive, King Edward VI School, Stratford-upon Avon, *Galatea* Box 1. n. p.

Mills, Perry. '*Antonio's Revenge*: Director's Copy of Script'. 2010. Edwards Boys Archive, King Edward VI School, Stratford-upon-Avon, *Antonio's Revenge* Folder 1.

Collection of photocopied images and sketches with annotations for *Dido, Queen of Carthage*. June 2013. Edward's Boys Archive, King Edward VI School, Stratford-upon-Avon, *Dido, Queen of Carthage* Box 1.

'Director's Ramblings'. *When Paul's Boys Met Edward's Boys* Programme. Edward's Boys, 2018. Edward's Boys Archive, King Edward VI School, Stratford-upon Avon, *When Paul's Boys Met Edward's Boys* Box 1. n. p.

'*Grobiana's Nuptials* – Big Meeting and First Rehearsal'. 2016. Edward's Boys Archive, King Edward VI School, Stratford-upon-Avon, *Grobiana's Nuptials* Box 1.

'*The Lady's Trial* at the SWP, 25th to 27th September 2015. INFORMATION TO PARENTS'. 2015. Edward's Boys Archive, King Edward VI School, Stratford-upon-Avon, *The Lady's Trial* Box 1.

'Sunday 14th February: LFH'. 2016. Edward's Boys Archive, King Edward VI School, Stratford-upon-Avon, *The Woman Hater* Box 1.

'Sunday 8th March – To Do'. 2015. Edward's Boys Archive, King Edward VI School, Stratford-upon-Avon, *The Lady's Trial* Box 1.

'WH Notes'. 2015. Edward's Boys Archive, King Edward VI School, Stratford-upon-Avon, *The Woman Hater* Box 1.

'*The Woman Hater*: Director's Copy of Script'. 2016. Edward's Boys Archive, King Edward VI School, Stratford-upon-Avon, *The Woman Hater* Folder 1.

'*The Woman in the Moon*: Director's Copy of Script'. 2018. Edward's Boys Archive, King Edward VI School, Stratford-upon-Avon, *The Woman in the Moon* Box 1.

Pocknell, Joe. 'Information Sheet for *The Lady's Trial*'. 2014. Edward's Boys Archive, King Edward VI School, Stratford-upon-Avon, *The Lady's Trial* Box 1.

Scragg, Leah. Letter to Perry Mills. 2018. Edward's Boys Archive, King Edward VI School, Stratford-upon-Avon, *The Woman in the Moon* Box 2.

Other Works

'Academic Curriculum'. *King Edward VI School: Shakespeare's School*, King Edward VI School, 2020, www.kes.net/academic-curriculum/. Accessed 7 July 2020.

Ackroyd, Julie. *Child Actors on the London Stage circa 1600: Their Education, Recruitment and Theatrical Success*. Sussex Academic Press, 2017.

'Admissions Policy'. *King Edward VI School: Shakespeare's School*, King Edward VI School, 2020, www.kes.net/admissions/. Accessed 7 July 2020.

Aebischer, Pascale. *Screening Early Modern Drama: Beyond Shakespeare*. Cambridge University Press, 2013. doi:10.1017/CBO9781139176194

Aebischer, Pascale, and Kathryn Prince, editors. *Performing Early Modern Drama Today*. Cambridge University Press, 2012. doi:10.1017/CBO9781139047975

Antonio's Revenge. Directed by Perry Mills, Gavin Birkett for King Edward VI School, 2011. DVD.

Bedau, Dani, and D. J. Hopkins. 'The Shakespeare Laboratory: Intercepting "Authenticity" through Research, Pedagogy, and Performance'. *Theatre Topics*, vol. 23, no. 2, 2013, pp. 145–56. doi:10.1353/tt.2013.0015

Bevington, David, Martin Butler, and Ian Donaldson, editors. *The Cambridge Edition of the Works of Ben Jonson*, vol. 2. Cambridge University Press, 2012.

Billing, Christian. 'Rehearsing Shakespeare: Embodiment, Collaboration, Risk and Play . . .'. *Shakespeare Bulletin*, vol. 30, no. 4, 2012, pp. 383–410. doi:10.1353/shb.2012.0072

Bowers, Fredson, editor. *The Dramatic Works in the Beaumont and Fletcher Canon*, vol. 1. Cambridge University Press, 1966.

Bowie-Sell, Daisy. 'Trevor Nunn: "If I Wasn't a Director for a Job, I Would Do It As a Hobby"'. *WhatsOnStage*, 14 March 2018, www.whatsonstage.com/bath-theatre/news/trevor-nunn-agnes-colander-interview-director_46025.html. Accessed 12 February 2020.

'The Boy Players – Extended'. *YouTube*, uploaded by uniwarwick, 29 November 2011, www.youtube.com/watch?v=bBXrB0bEO34.

Boys' Companies Present Marston: 'The History of Antonio and Mellida' (Acts I & II), Dulwich College; 'The Dutch Courtesan' (Up to & inc. Act III Sc. i), King Edward VI School. Gavin Birkett for King Edward VI School, 2008.

Britland, Karen, editor. *'The Dutch Courtesan' by John Marston*. Bloomsbury, 2018.

Brown, Karin. 'Appendix 1: Professional Productions of Early Modern Drama in the UK and USA, 1960–2010'. *Performing Early Modern Drama Today*, edited by Pascale Aebischer and Kathryn Prince. Cambridge University Press, 2012, pp. 178–217. doi:10.1017/CBO9781139047975.011

Carlson, Marvin. *The Haunted Stage: The Theatre As Memory Machine*. University of Michigan Press, 2003.

Carroll, Tim, Emma Smith, and Martin White. 'Purposeful Playing? Purposeful Criticism?'. *Shakespeare, Language and the Stage: The Fifth Wall: Approaches to Shakespeare from Criticism, Performance and Theatre Studies*, edited by Lynette Hunter and Peter Lichtenfels. Bloomsbury, 2005, pp. 38–60.

Cave, Richard Allen. 'The Value of Practical Work and of Theatregoing in the Study of Seventeenth-Century Drama (1600–1640)'. *Literature Compass*, vol. 1, no. 1, 2003, n. p. doi:10.1111/j.1741-4113.2004.00110_1_1.x

A Chaste Maid in Cheapside. Directed by Perry Mills, Gavin Birkett for King Edward VI School, 2010. DVD.

The Complete Works of John Marston. University of Leeds, 2020, https://johnmarston.leeds.ac.uk/. Accessed 22 April 2020.

Conkie, Rob. *The Globe Theatre Project: Shakespeare and Authenticity*. Edwin Mellen Press, 2006.

'Rehearsal: The Pleasures of the Flesh'. *Shakespeare Bulletin*, vol. 30, no. 4, 2012, pp. 411–29. doi:10.1353/shb.2012.0077

Connerton, Paul. *How Societies Remember*. Cambridge University Press, 1989. doi:10.1017/CBO9780511628061

Davies, Callan. '*The Woman in the Moon*: In Conversation with Edward's Boys'. *Before Shakespeare*, 13 March 2018, https://beforeshakespeare.com/2018/03/13/the-woman-in-the-moon-in-conversation-with-edwards-boys/. Accessed 19 February 2020.

Davies, Harry. 'Look Back in Gender'. *Edward's Boys*, King Edward VI School, 2016, http://edwardsboys.org/look-back-in-gender/. Accessed 7 February 2020.

Davis, Jim, Katie Normington, Gilli Bush-Bailey, and Jacky Bratton. 'Researching Theatre History and Historiography: Research Methods and Methodology'. *Research Methods in Theatre and Performance*, edited by Baz Kershaw and Helen Nicholson. Edinburgh University Press, 2011, pp. 86–110.

Dessen, Alan C. '"Original Practices" at the Globe: A Theatre Historian's View'. *Shakespeare's Globe: A Theatrical Experiment*, edited by Christie Carson and Farah Karim-Cooper. Cambridge University Press, 2008, pp. 45–53.

Eagleton, Terry. *Criticism and Ideology: A Study in Marxist Literary Theory*. Verso, 1978.

Edward's Boys. King Edward VI School, 2020, http://edwardsboys.org/. Accessed 7 February 2020.

Edward's Boys Film Extracts, Gavin Birkett for King Edward VI School, 2015. DVD.

Edwards, Henry. Personal interview. 4 June 2018.

Elizabethan Boy Players: The Thisby Project. Directed by Perry Mills and Carol Chillington Rutter, Gavin Birkett for King Edward VI School, 2005. DVD.

Evans, Mark. *Performance, Movement and the Body*. Red Globe Press, 2019.

'Expert Opinion'. *Edward's Boys*, King Edward VI School, 2016, edwards-boys.org/expert-opinion. Accessed 7 February 2020.

'Extra-Curricular'. *King Edward VI School: Shakespeare's School*, King Edward VI School, 2020, www.kes.net/extra-curricular/. Accessed 7 July 2020.

Feuillerat, Albert, editor. *Documents Relating to the Revels at Court in the Time of King Edward VI and Queen Mary*. A. Uystpruyst, 1914.

'The Ford Experiment and Boy Players at Shakespeare's Globe'. *Theatre Voice*, 11 October 2015, www.theatrevoice.com/audio/ford-experiment-shakespeares-globe/. Accessed 7 February 2020.

Galatea. Directed by Perry Mills, Gavin Birkett for King Edward VI School, 2014.

Garner, Stanton B., Jr. *Bodied Spaces: Phenomenology and Performance in Contemporary Drama*. Cornell University Press, 1994.

Gill, Roma, editor. *The Complete Works of Christopher Marlowe*, vol. 1. Clarendon, 1987.

Gopsill, Rory. Personal interview. 7 June 2018.

Grobiana's Nuptials. Directed by Perry Mills, Gavin Birkett for King Edward VI School, 2016.

Gunby, David, David Carnegie, and MacDonald P. Jackson, editors. *The Works of John Webster*, vol. 4. Cambridge University Press, 2019.

Hardy, Adam. Personal interview. 4 July 2018.

Hatch, Fin, George Hodson, Dan Power, Dan Wilkinson, and James Williams. 'Exit, Pursued by a Bear . . .'. *Edward's Boys*, King Edward

VI School, 2016, http://edwardsboys.org/old-boys/exit-pursued-by
-a-bear/. Accessed 7 February 2018.

Hawkins, Jack. Personal interview. 4 July 2018.

Henry V. Directed by Perry Mills, Gavin Birkett for King Edward VI
School, 2013. DVD.

Heron, Jonathan, Nicholas Monk, and Paul Prescott. 'Letting the Dead
Come Out to Dance: An Embodied and Spatial Approach to Teaching
Early Modern Drama'. *Performing Early Modern Drama Today*, edited
by Pascale Aebischer and Kathryn Prince. Cambridge University
Press, 2012, pp. 162–77. doi:10.1017/CBO9781139047975.010

Hewison, Robert, John Holden, and Samuel Jones. *All Together: A Creative
Approach to Organisational Change*. Demos, 2010.

Hirsch, Brett D. 'Review: *Dido, Queen of Carthage*'. *Edward's Boys*, King
Edward VI School, 2016, http://edwardsboys.org/reviews-and-feed
back/review-dido-queen-of-carthage/. Accessed 7 February 2020.

Hodgdon, Barbara. 'Rehearsal Process As Critical Practice: John Barton's 1978
Love's Labour's Lost'. *Theatre History Studies*, vol. 8, 1988, pp. 11–34.

Shakespeare, Performance and the Archive. Routledge, 2016.

Jackson, MacDonald P., and Michael Neill, editors. *The Selected Plays of
John Marston*. Cambridge University Press, 1986.

'job, n. 2'. *OED Online*, Oxford University Press, March 2019, www
.oed.com/view/Entry/101396. Accessed 25 March 2020.

Jowett, John. 'Review: *A Chaste Maid in Cheapside*'. *Edward's Boys*, King
Edward VI School, 2016, http://edwardsboys.org/reviews-and-feed
back/review-a-chaste-maid-in-cheapside/. Accessed 7 February 2020.

Kathman, David. 'John Rice and the Boys of the Jacobean King's Men'.
Shakespeare Survey, vol. 68, 2015, pp. 247–66. doi:10.1017/
CBO9781316258736.020

Kesson, Andy. 'Review: *Galatea*'. *Edward's Boys*, King Edward VI School, 2016, http://edwardsboys.org/reviews-and-feedback/review-galatea/. Accessed 7 February 2018.

'Women in the Moons'. *Before Shakespeare*, 10 March 2018, https://beforeshakespeare.com/2018/03/10/women-in-the-moons/. Accessed 7 February 2020.

Kirwan, Peter. 'Not-Shakespeare and the Shakespearean Ghost'. *The Oxford Handbook of Shakespeare and Performance*, edited by James C. Bulman, Oxford University Press, 2017, pp. 87–103. doi:10.1093/oxfordhb9780199687169.013.19

'Review: *Antonio's Revenge* (Edward's Boys) @ King Edward VI Grammar School'. The *Bardathon*, University of Nottingham, 11 March 2011, http://blogs.nottingham.ac.uk/bardathon/2011/03/11/antonios-revenge-edwards-boys-king-edward-vi-grammar-school/. Accessed 19 February 2020.

'Review: *Henry V* (Edward's Boys) @ The Swan, Stratford-upon-Avon'. *The Bardathon*, University of Nottingham, 18 March 2013, http://blogs.nottingham.ac.uk/bardathon/2013/03/18/henry-v-edwards-boysthe-swan-stratford-upon-avon/. Accessed 19 February 2020.

Shakespeare in the Theatre: Cheek by Jowl. Bloomsbury, 2019.

The Lady's Trial. Directed by Perry Mills, Gavin Birkett for King Edward VI School, 2015. DVD.

Leslie, Struan. 'On Movement-Based Theatre'. *DigitalTheatre+*, 2014, www.digitaltheatreplus.com/education/collections/digital-theatre/on-movement-based-theatre-struan-leslie. Accessed 2 March 2020.

Personal interview. 13 March 2020.

'Struan's Work'. *Struanleslie.com*, 2020, www.struanleslie.com/work. Accessed 3 March 2020.

Lopez, Jeremy. 'Appendix 3: Performances of Early Modern Plays by Amateur and Student Groups since 1887'. *Performing Early Modern Drama Today*, edited by Pascale Aebischer and Kathryn Prince. Cambridge University Press, 2012, pp. 225–7. doi:10.1017/CBO9781139047975.013

'The Seeds of Time: Student Theatre and the Drama of Shakespeare's Contemporaries'. *Performing Early Modern Drama Today*, edited by Pascale Aebischer and Kathryn Prince. Cambridge University Press, 2012, pp. 35–52. doi:10.1017/CBO9781139047975.003

Maguire, Laurie. 'Company Profile'. *Edward's Boys*, King Edward VI School, 2019, http://edwardsboys.org/profile/. Accessed 15 March 2020.

Maguire, Laurie, and Emma Smith. '"Time's Comic Sparks": The Dramaturgy of *A Mad World, My Masters* and *Timon of Athens*'. *The Oxford Handbook of Thomas Middleton*, edited by Gary Taylor and Trish Thomas Henley. Oxford University Press, 2012, pp. 181–95. doi:10.1093/oxfordhb/9780199559886.013.0012

The Malcontent. Directed by Perry Mills, 30 March 2019, Trinity College Hall, Oxford. Performance.

McAuley, Gay. *Not Magic but Work: An Ethnographic Account of a Rehearsal Process*. Manchester University Press, 2012.

McCarthy, Harry R. 'Review: *When Paul's Boys Met Edward's Boys*'. *Edward's Boys*, King Edward VI School, 2018, http://edwardsboys.org/review-pauls-boys-met-edwards-boys/. Accessed 12 February 2020.

'Review of *Summer's Last Will and Testament*, directed by Perry Mills.' *Shakespeare Bulletin*, vol. 36, no. 2, 2018, pp. 326–31. doi:10.1353/shb.2018.0028

'Review of *The Woman Hater*, directed by Perry Mills.' *Shakespeare Bulletin*, vol. 34, no. 4, 2016, pp. 719–23. doi:10.1353/shb.2016.0063

'The One That Got Away; or, The Almost Silent Woman.' *Soundcloud*, 1 May 2020, https://soundcloud.com/user-999191870/the-one-that-got-away-or-the-almost-silent-woman. Accessed 6 July 2020.

Menzer, Paul. 'Afterword: Discovery Spaces? Research at the Globe and Blackfriars'. *Inside Shakespeare: Essays on the Blackfriars Stage*, edited by Paul Menzer. Susquehanna University Press, 2006, pp. 223–30.

    Shakespeare in the Theatre: The American Shakespeare Center. Bloomsbury, 2017.

Mills, Alex. 'What Has Edward's Boys Ever Done for Us?' *Edward's Boys*, King Edward VI School, 2010, http://edwardsboys.org/old-boys/what-has-edwards-boys-ever-done-for-us/. Accessed 12 February 2020.

Mills, Perry. Personal interview. 3 July 2018.

    Personal interview. 3 February 2020.

    'Re: Edward's Boys'. Received by Harry R. McCarthy, 28 June 2017.

    'Re: Rehearsals'. Received by Harry R. McCarthy, 8 January 2020.

Mills, Perry, and Alex Mills. 'In the Company of Edward's Boys'. *Drama and Pedagogy in Medieval and Early Modern England*, edited by Elisabeth Dutton and James McBain. Narr, 2015, pp. 275–93.

Mitchell, Jamie. Personal interview. 3 July 2018.

Mother Bombie. Directed by Perry Mills, Gavin Birkett for King Edward VI School, 2010. DVD.

Nagar, Ritvick. Personal interview. 2 February 2020.

Nicholson, Helen, Nadine Holdsworth, and Jane Milling. *The Ecologies of Amateur Theatre*. Palgrave Macmillan, 2018.

Nora, Pierre. 'Between Memory and History: *Les Lieux de Mémoire*'. *Representations*, vol. 26, no. 1, 1989, pp. 7–25. doi:10.2307/2928520

Palfrey, Simon, and Tiffany Stern. *Shakespeare in Parts*. Oxford University Press, 2007. doi:10.1093/acprof:oso/9780199272051.001.0001

Pearson, Mike, and Michael Shanks. *Theatre/Archaeology*. Routledge, 2001.

Pérez Díez, José A. 'Review of *The Malcontent*'. *Edward's Boys*, King Edward VI School, 2019, http://edwardsboys.org/review-of-the-malcontent-by-dr-jose-a-perez-diez/. Accessed 15 March 2020.

Performing Dido. *Vimeo*, uploaded by Dollar Bet Productions, 2015. https://vimeo.com/126939242.

Performing Dido: Edward's Boys and Early Drama Oxford. Gavin Birkett for King Edward VI School, 2013.

Pocknell, Joe. Personal interview. 4 July 2018.

Pollick, Michael. 'What Is a Cold Open?' *wiseGeek*, 2020, www.wisegeek.com/what-is-a-cold-open.htm. Accessed 10 March 2020.

Price, Eoin. 'Monsters'. *Aside Notes*, 16 March 2014, https://asidenotes.wordpress.com/2014/03/16/monsters/. Accessed 7 February 2020.

Purcell, Stephen. 'Practice-as-Research and Original Practices'. *Shakespeare Bulletin*, vol. 35, no. 3, 2017, pp. 425–43. doi:10.1353/shb.2017.0033

Radosavljević, Duška. 'Snapshot #2: Michael Boyd on the RSC Ensemble'. *Encountering Ensemble*, edited by John Britton. Methuen, 2013, pp. 147–51.

Research in Action: The Marston Project. Directed by Perry Mills, 22 July 2017, Sam Wanamaker Playhouse, London. Performance.

Roach, Joseph R. *Cities of the Dead: Circum-Atlantic Performance*. Columbia University Press, 1996.

Rokison, Abigail. *Shakespearean Verse Speaking: Text and Theatre Practice*. Cambridge University Press, 2009.

Rutter, Carol Chillington. 'Learning Thisby's Part – or – What's Hecuba to Him?' *Shakespeare Bulletin*, vol. 22, no. 3, 2004, pp. 5–30.

'Playing with Boys on Middleton's Stage: and Ours'. *The Oxford Handbook of Thomas Middleton*, edited by Gary Taylor and Trish Thomas Henley. Oxford University Press, 2012, pp. 98–115. doi:10.1093/oxfordhb/9780199559886.013.0007

Sah, Nilay. Personal interview. 2 February 2020.

Schneider, Rebecca. *Performing Remains: Art and War in Times of Theatrical Reenactment*. Routledge, 2011.

References

Scragg, Leah, editor. *'The Woman in the Moon': By John Lyly*, Manchester University Press, 2006.

'Shakespeare in the Theatre'. *Bloomsbury.com*, 2020, www.bloomsbury.com /uk/series/shakespeare-in-the-theatre/. Accessed 12 February 2020.

Sharp, Tom. 'The Spirit of Edward's Boys: "Just Do It!" *Edward's Boys*, King Edward VI School, 2016, http://edwardsboys.org/old-boys/ the-spirit-of-edwards-boys-just-do-it/. Accessed 7 February 2018.

Singh, Anita. 'Drama School Students Need More Shakespeare Training, Says RSC Boss'. *The Telegraph*, 4 February 2020, www.telegraph.co .uk/news/2020/02/04/drama-school-students-need-shakespeare- training-says-rsc-boss/. Accessed 4 February 2020.

Smith, Emma. 'Review: *Henry V*'. *Edward's Boys*, King Edward VI School, 2016, http://edwardsboys.org/reviews-and-feedback/review-henry -v/. Accessed 7 February 2020.

Smith, Emma, editor. *Shakespeare in Production: King Henry V*. Cambridge University Press, 2002.

'Sport'. *King Edward VI School: Shakespeare's School*, King Edward VI School, 2020, www.kes.net/extra-curricular/sport/. Accessed 7 July 2020.

Stern, Tiffany. *Rehearsal from Shakespeare to Sheridan*. Clarendon, 2000. doi:10.1093/acprof:oso/9780199229727.001.0001

Summer's Last Will and Testament. Directed by Perry Mills, 29 September 2017, Sam Wanamaker Playhouse, London. Performance.

Taylor, Diana. *The Archive and the Repertoire: Performing Cultural Memory in the Americas*. Duke University Press, 2003.

Taylor, Gary, and John Lavagnino, editors. *Thomas Middleton: The Collected Works*. Oxford University Press, 2007. doi:10.1093/ actrade/9780199580538.book.1

The Thomas Nashe Project. Newcastle University, 2020, https://research .ncl.ac.uk/thethomasnasheproject/. Accessed 22 April 2020.

'A Time of Revolution'. *In Search of Shakespeare*, devised and presented by Michael Wood, 2 Entertain Video, 2003.

Tribble, Evelyn. *Cognition in the Globe: Attention and Memory in Shakespeare's Theatre*. Palgrave Macmillan, 2011.

A Trick to Catch the Old One. Directed by Perry Mills, 9 March 2017, Simpkins Lee Theatre, Oxford. Performance.

Tunstall, Darren. 'Shakespeare and the Lecoq Tradition'. *Shakespeare Bulletin*, vol. 30, no. 4, 2012, pp. 469–84. doi:10.1353/shb.2012.0092

Twycross, Meg. 'John Redford, *Wit and Science*.' *The Oxford Handbook of Tudor Drama*, edited by Thomas Betteridge and Greg Walker. Oxford University Press, 2012, pp. 224–38.

Unperfect Actors: Extracts from the Works of William Shakespeare. Directed by Perry Mills, Gavin Birkett for King Edward VI School, 2016.

Van Es, Bart. *Shakespeare in Company*. Oxford University Press, 2013. doi:10.1093/acprof:oso/9780199569311.001.0001

Vogiaridis, Pascal. Personal interview. 4 July 2018.

Waters, Charlie. Personal interview. 4 July 2018.

Weimann, Robert. *Author's Pen and Actor's Voice: Playing and Writing in Shakespeare's Theatre*. Edited by Helen Higbee and William N. West. Cambridge University Press, 2000. doi:10.1017/CBO9780511484070

Weingust, Don. 'Authentic Performances or Performances of Authenticity? Original Practices and the Repertory Schedule'. *Shakespeare*, vol. 10, no. 4, 2014, pp. 402–10. doi:10.1080/17450918.2014.889205

Westward Ho! Directed by Perry Mills, Gavin Birkett for King Edward VI School, 2012. DVD.

When Paul's Boys Met Edward's Boys. Directed by Perry Mills, 25 and 26 June 2018, St Paul's Cathedral and Sam Wanamaker Playhouse, London. Performances.

Wickham, Glynne, Herbert Berry, and William Ingram. *English Professional Theatre, 1530–1660*. Cambridge University Press, 2000.

Wiggins, Martin, in association with Catherine Richardson. *British Drama 1533–1642: A Catalogue*. Oxford University Press, 2012—. 10 vols.

Wilkinson, Dan. Personal interview. 11 June 2018.

Will at Westminster. Directed by Perry Mills, 30 April 2016, Westminster Hall, London. Performance.

Wit and Science. Directed by Perry Mills, 8 July 2019, New College Chapel, Oxford. Performance.

The Woman Hater. Directed by Perry Mills, 10 March 2016, Oxford University Catholic Chaplaincy, Oxford. Performance.

The Woman in the Moon. Directed by Perry Mills, 8 March 2018, Simpkins Lee Theatre, Oxford. Performance.

Worthen, W. B. *Shakespeare and the Authority of Performance*. Cambridge University Press, 1997. doi:10.1017/CBO9780511583193

Shakespeare and the Force of Modern Performance. Cambridge University Press, 2003. doi:10.1017/CBO978051148408

Acknowledgments

I am grateful to Bill Worthen and the two anonymous readers of this Element for their unusually thoughtful feedback. The research that underpins this Element was made possible thanks to grants from the Society for Theatre Research and the South, West, and Wales Doctoral Training Partnership (funded by the Arts and Humanities Research Council). Many thanks to those friends and colleagues who have kindly discussed Edward's Boys productions, and my work on the company, with me: Pascale Aebischer, Emma Benton, Robbie Hand, Hester Lees-Jeffries, Clare McManus, Jane Milling, Lucy Munro, Esther Osorio Whewell, José A. Pérez Díez, Lois Potter, Eleanor Rycroft, Bailey Sincox, Emma Smith, and Tiffany Stern. The extraordinary Edward's Boys company members past and present have been generous with their time, and I wish in particular to thank those who gave permission for their words to be reproduced here: Henry Edwards, Rory Gopsill, Will Groves, Adam Hardy, Jack Hawkins, Felix Kerrison-Adams, Jamie Mitchell, Ritvick Nagar, Joe Pocknell, Nilay Sah, Pascal Vogiaridis, Charlie Waters, and Dan Wilkinson. Struan Leslie, Louisa Nightingale, Richard Pearson, and Suzie Vogiaridis also provided essential help with my research on the company. This Element is dedicated, with a 'perfectly adequate' amount of affection, to Perry Mills.

Cambridge Elements

Shakespeare Performance

W. B. Worthen
Barnard College

W. B. Worthen is Alice Brady Pels Professor in the Arts, and Chair of the Theatre Department at Barnard College. He is also co-chair of the Ph.D. Program in Theatre at Columbia University, where he is Professor of English and Comparative Literature.

About the Series

Shakespeare Performance is a dynamic collection in a field that is both always emerging and always evanescent. Responding to the global range of Shakespeare performance today, the series launches provocative, urgent criticism for researchers, graduate students and practitioners. Publishing scholarship with a direct bearing on the contemporary contexts of Shakespeare performance, it considers specific performances, material and social practices, ideological and cultural frameworks, emerging and significant artists and performance histories.

Cambridge Elements

Shakespeare Performance

Printed in the United States
By Bookmasters